S0-ABZ-954

DATE DUE

FEB 1 1 1970

JUN 2 1970

JAN 1971

AUG 2 5 1971

THE
SOCIAL
MATRIX
OF
PHYSICAL
EDUCATION

Prentice-Hall Foundations of Physical Education Series

JOHN E. NIXON
Stanford University
Series Editor

THE
SOCIAL
MATRIX
OF
PHYSICAL
EDUCATION

Celeste Ulrich
University of North Carolina, Greensboro

PRENTICE-HALL, INC., ENGLEWOOD CLIFFS, NEW JERSEY

© 1968 by Prentice-Hall, Inc., Englewood Cliffs, New Jersey

All rights reserved. No part of this book may be reproduced
in any form or by any means without permission in writing
from the publisher.

Printed in the United States of America
Library of Congress Catalog Card No. 68-18593
Current printing (last digit): 10   9   8   7   6   5   4   3   2   1

PRENTICE-HALL INTERNATIONAL, INC., *London*
PRENTICE-HALL OF AUSTRALIA, PTY. LTD., *Sydney*
PRENTICE-HALL OF CANADA, LTD., *Toronto*
PRENTICE-HALL OF INDIA PRIVATE LTD., *New Delhi*
PRENTICE-HALL OF JAPAN, INC., *Tokyo*

HM
66
2145

Hd13ta69

####X
5X

To

Gail Hennis

master of interaction

and

Lyda Gordon Shivers

practical social theorist

Series Preface

The purpose of the *Foundations of Physical Education* series is to provide a set of textbooks which, by presenting selected generalizations from related fields of knowledge, contribute to a sophisticated understanding of physical education as an academic discipline. These validated generalizations provide a sound basis for educational decision-making by teachers, coaches, supervisors, and administrators at all school levels.

Physical education currently is defined as the art and science of voluntary, purposeful human movement. Its central concern is man engaging in selected motor performances and the meaning and significance of these experiences. Thus, physical education is a broad cross-disciplinary subject. It requires of its scholars and practitioners a command of the most relevant generalizations, being generated in the closely related disciplines, which describe and explain phenomena associated with human movement. Those disciplines which provide the most relevant foundational knowledge for physical education are physiology, neurology, psychology, sociology, anthropology, history, philosophy, anatomy, and kinesiology.

Present physical education texts generally fail to treat in depth relevant generalizations from related disciplines. In these books, one or two physical education authors have attempted to present a series of "principles" of physical education in a few chapters, each of which contains some reference to knowledge in various fields. In today's world of rapidly expanding knowledge, one or two authors can no longer be well versed in several disciplines sufficiently to write principles and foundations books in physical education, which possess the depth and sophistication required to understand and describe the field, and to guide its practices.

With rare exceptions, scholars of other disciplines have not devoted their major attention to investigation and reports which concern physical education phenomena. Thus, for example, the historians have virtually neglected the history of sport in general history books and few sociologists have studied sports as their major line of inquiry.

Nonetheless a vast accumulation of knowledge exists in the literature of the foundation fields which has direct and essential relevance to physical education. Most of this knowledge has not been accumulated systematically or reported and interpreted accurately to the physical education profession. The task of selecting and reporting relevant generalizations from any one discipline requires a physical education scholar who is also a scholar of the related subject.

For the first time in physical education literature, this series incorporates books about physical education, prepared by distinguished physical education scholars, who have established reputations for knowledge and competence in the subject matter and in the principal modes of inquiry in the related fields. Thus, each volume synthesizes recent knowledge into usable form for students and teachers and is unique in physical education literature. Furthermore, the reader is instructed in the process of developing his own *principles* of physical education from his increasing knowledge and understanding. Comprehensive bibliographies list basic references for further study in each field.

This series is appropriate for Foundations or Principles of Physical Education courses at both the undergraduate and graduate levels. Individual volumes are suitable for courses concerning their respective subject areas. Also, these books are valuable for collateral reading and can provide the basis for individual study projects.

The series provides a reference source for the latest knowledge of scientific, behavioral, and humanistic insight and understanding, which constitute the subject and the practice of physical education today. It belongs in the library of every student and teacher of physical education.

J. N.

Preface

Physical education is a maverick discipline, which draws freely from the knowledge of the biological, physical, and behavioral sciences. It also finds its meaning in philosophy, aesthetics, and the liberal arts. The disciplinary integrity of physical education is based upon human movement, and it is to that point of reference that the physical educator relates all knowledge.

The discipline has probed deeply into the biological nature of moving man, but has been a little nonchalant with regard to the understandings suggested by the behavioral sciences, especially sociology and social anthropology.

This volume, written for professional students in physical education, presents some of the basic elements involved in the interaction of mobile man. It attempts to find reference for physical education. Hopefully, it can serve as a textbook in applied sociology.

All references have been combined into a large bibliography which will be found at the end of the text. Specific references are cited throughout the text, by date of the reference and page number of a quotation.

No work is ever the creation of one person. The interaction that shapes an individual's thoughts, attitudes, and beliefs creates life-long obligations and responsibilities.

My own obligations for this book are many. Eleanor Metheny has been a well-spring of professional understanding, enthusiasm, and challenge for many years, and my debt to her is beyond repayment.

Ethel Martus and the staff of physical educators at the University of North Carolina at Greensboro have lent me both scholarly and emotional support at times when I needed such. Their belief and understanding has provided a sense of security and well-being.

Delbert Oberteuffer, Caroline Sinclair, Arthur Esslinger, Ellen Griffin, Minnie Lynn, and Catherine Allen have always found the time to question, explore, and adventure with shared ideas.

My keenest sense of responsibility and obligation is to the men and women whom I have had the privilege of teaching. They have challenged me with their thinking; they have cast doubt on my absolutes; they have given substance to my relatives. For this particular work, I am in special debt to Dorothy Richardson and Waneen Wyrick. Dorothy has provided me with insights and understandings about the cultural heritage of America, which could have been seen only through the eyes of a former Scot who is impassioned with her adopted home. Waneen has been the distant, ever probing skeptic who is never satisfied with any idea for fear that it has not been explored fully.

Finally, it is to Gail Hennis and Lyda Gordon Shivers that my attempt to study the social matrix of physical education is dedicated. Dr. Shivers is the personification of the worth of social interaction and Gail has faith and understands.

C. U.

Contents

THE

SOCIAL

MATRIX

OF

PHYSICAL

EDUCATION

I

Social Bases
of Human Behavior

"How about a game!"

Human mobility is the dominant design in the pattern which spans life and death. Movement always can be identified in biological terms, but the meaning of human mobility is best interpreted in ways other than biological. Movement has social implications. Man does not move irrationally. He moves with purpose and his purpose serves to identify his needs, desires, and nature. Human mobility is a part of the orderly matrix which gives meaning to life. Hence Metheny's fundamental suggestion that as we learn to move, so we move to learn (1965).

There are few, if any, sleazy threads in nature's pattern, for each thread has its integrity, its function, and its design potential. As Herrick has suggested, "The most fundamental law of nature revealed by modern science is that our cosmos is an integrated, orderly system of natural processes that are self-sustaining and self-regulating (1956, p. 42).

Human mobility is human behavior. It is every student's obligation to study the warp and woof of this phenomenon and attempt to recognize the patterning that comprises human life. In a sense, the study of man and his behavior is the property of all disciplines, but the special property of the behavioral sciences. In a very real sense, the study of the mobile behavior of man is the unique function of physical education.

Physical education must turn to the behavioral sciences to find the rationale for human behavior. We know that behavior is not capricious; it is predictable. Thus, if we study the design of the human pattern, we will be able better to understand and educate man.

First the student of human nature must look for the organizational pattern in man's behavior, for organization is essential to sustain life itself. An organizational scheme provides a

1

degree of certainty about a phenomenon, it tends to create the power of understanding, and it provides the continuity upon which analysis can be based.

We might find an analogy for the search for organization by comparing it to the simplest identification of a game. If you should see a group of people running helter-skelter within an area, you might suspect you were viewing a snake pit of disorganization. But once you begin to find a pattern for the running and note that there is one person who must do the catching and the tagging, then the apparently pointless running begins to make sense. You see that the rest of the group is running away from "It" and that the group has boundaries in which it is allowed to move. You identify the running game as Tag. Once the understanding of the organization has been made, it is possible to predict what the subsequent behavior will be; you understand why people run and from whom they run. In the prediction of future behavior, there is inference for understanding, control, and education.

It would seem that individual psychology should be able to account for all that man does, were it not for the fact that man does not live by himself. He lives as a part of a group and in that group there is social organization and interaction. The organizational groups of man have identity, as does man himself, and so it is necessary for us to turn to the science of human relationships to better understand the meaning of human movement in its fullest context.

Man is continually seeking to serve his individual interests as well as those of the groups of which he is a part. The sciences of sociology and social anthropology identify those interests and attempt to analyze them.

When the school boy turns to his classmate and makes the suggestion, "How about a game?" he has unconsciously created a model of the social base of human behavior. Games are built upon social interpretation of movement and thus lend lucidity to the concept of moving to learn as one learns to move.

SOCIALIZED MAN

Man never exists as a single individual, alone and unrelated to others. Anderson and Parker have pointed out that life "is a natural process of continuous activity in and through the forms of human association in our society" (1964, p. 4). A human society is the most basic, the most generalized, the most inclusive of all relationship structures.

Societies are formed because individuals have needs which are best met by the organization of groups of men. Man possesses a social need which suggests that kind look for kind. This need is evidenced in the fact that humans seek sociability and sympathy, and they have found that these attitudes may best be gained from other humans. As Cooley says, "Self and society go together, as phases of a common whole" (*Social Organization*, 1920, p. 8).

When a child is born he immediately becomes a part of a human group, even if that group is the simple dyad of mother and child. Usually the relationship is more complex, with a family unit of parents, brothers, sisters, grandparents, and a bevy of uncles, aunts, and cousins all making the new-born individual welcome to his new society.

characteristics of a society

Societal structure usually follows certain prescribed patterns of identification. It can be expected that most societies will involve large numbers of people, will be situated in a definite geographical area, will have planned systems of association, will foster reciprocal relationships, will cooperate if possible, will accept mutual interests and goals, will develop a sense of sharing, and will possess established norms and interrelated statuses. There are certain ties which have a tendency to bind men together in a society. The needs for communication and trophallaxis (the care and nurture of each other) have special magnetic powers in the formulation of a society.

Thus, the newborn child is immediately confronted with his relatives, all of whom reside in his recognition world. He quickly discerns his relationship with those relatives, recognizing the roles that each relative plays. He knows that mother is the provider of food and comfort, father offers protection and shelter, brothers and sisters are rivals and friends, and the rest of the community of people have a special role in relation to their interest in him.

man's responsibility to society

Man creates his society for his own good, but after the creation, he must assume responsibility for that which he has created. Society is not static but dynamic, and it is up to man to guide the dynamics of his institution. Thus, as society evolves, it grows in complexity, it fosters integration patterns, and it seeks simplicity through specialization. To all of these trends, individual man has an obligation—an obligation of understanding and direction.

Hence, when physical educators look at the movement of man, they cannot view his mobility in a vacuum of self; they must consider the social meaning of that movement, the things that influenced it, and the understandings that accrue from it. Man's sense of his responsibility to society determines the depth of his understandings, and his education is based upon such depth.

the study of society

The fields of sociology and social anthropology seek to study the associations of man with man. They attempt to understand human relationships and the institutions which control those relationships. It is important to acknowledge that these behavioral sciences are fields of knowledge and not reform movements. They study what *is*, letting the chips fall as they may. The study of society is an amoral study, for science does not attempt to place value judgments upon its findings.

Hence, as physical educators find meaning for movement within the social structure, they must realize that they are not attempting to designate values. They just hope to expose facts.

The science of human relationships deals with purposive behavior, for man can envision goals and initiate actions. Hence it is important for physical educators to avoid the temptation to make value judgments about the findings within the social concept of movement.

EDUCATED MAN

Because society does not dare trust the responsibility of passing on its heritage to unorganized institutions, it charters education to train its members for the adult role, a role of performance. Thus, education has the sanction of society and acts as its archives. In addition, it becomes the role of education to act as the innovator of societal progress. Formal education then has the tremendous responsibility of society's past and its future.

Education produces philosophers and scientists; it produces humanitarians and technicians. The philosopher's duty is to make an inquiry into inquiry; the humanitarian seeks to humanize man via a relationship with the arts; the technician attempts to make operant the ideas and concepts of education; and the scientist is interested in prediction and control.

characteristics of education

Education has three precise responsibilities to society. First, it must pass on the heritage of the race and the culture; secondly, it must help man with his social adjustment; and thirdly, it must ascertain new relationships and create new knowledges.

All of the disciplines which fall under education are obliged to follow these directives, and physical education is one such discipline. Thus, as physical education seeks to fulfill its educational obligations, it must teach more than skill techniques, physical fitness, sportsmanship, good health habits, and rules and strategy. It must find its *raison d'être* within the context of the characteristics of general education.

stages of knowledge

Knowledge just does not appear in the educational process without discipline. It does not spring full grown from the head of Zeus and it is not automatically accepted. Most knowledge goes through what Rosenberg and Coser have called the law of three stages (1964).

The first stage is the theological, or fictitious, stage. At this point, knowledge is usually accepted because it is divine or because it is a part of a situation which has empirical verification. The second stage is the metaphysical, or abstract, stage, and here knowledge is accepted because it is a logical deduction or induction and because it need not be articulated, only recognized. The third stage of knowledge is the scientific, or positive, stage, and in this context facts have been scrutinized by a very exacting process and have been subjected to verification through the process of replication.

Education recognizes and identifies the various stages of knowledge with regard to any facet of human understanding. For example, the concept that love is good and a virtue has always had a theological flavor in the Golden Rule. The metaphysical and abstract understanding of love has dominated the literature of certain periods and has been used to describe abstractions of value, good and evil. Just recently we have ascertained that love is a positive value because it promotes growth, health, socialization, and behavioral homeostasis. We are daring to measure love by measuring the effects of love and the lack of love.

It should be emphasized that scientific investigation and positive discernment do not detract from a metaphysical or theological concept. Love can still carry the value of "good" and serve as the tenet of faith no matter how it is understood.

interdisciplinary approach to education

It used to be thought that real understanding of design integrity could only come as we dissected the fabric and saw what it was made of. It was believed that each discipline within education had a special way of looking at man and of identifying his nature. Thus, education grew up with a disciplinary context that still lingers today. More and more we are coming to believe that man can best be understood through an *interdisciplinary* approach, and we are daring to cross lines of inquiry that have never before been traversed. Anatomy seeks the aid of physiology to understand function, and thus we have functional anatomy and structural physiology. Psychology looks for neural understandings and we have physiological psychology. Sociology attempts to understand individual behavior and we have social psychology. Anthropology seeks the meaning of society in its study of man and we have social anthropology. There seems to be hope that education will turn to the behavioral sciences to augment the social sciences. Even the humanities seek a rationale in the physical and behavioral sciences as well as in the arts.

In this interdisciplinary approach to education, there have been many exciting constructs for physical education. Physical education, a maverick discipline, has traditionally sought its knowledges from the sciences, the arts, and the humanities. It now appears that physical education is emerging with its own rationale, a rationale which suggests that mobile man is the focal point of interest and that understandings of man in this capacity will cross disciplinary structures and offer new ideas and concepts to all of education.

PHYSICALLY EDUCATED MAN

Movement is a life concept as well as a behavior principle, and it affects all situations in which man finds himself. Man is dependent upon systemic movement for functional integrity and upon overt movement for his social and psychic behavior. Without movement, there is no life worthy of identification. It is to the concept of movement that physically educated man addresses himself.

responsibilities of physical education

Because physical education has been concerned traditionally with sports and games and cardio-respiratory integrity, it is well to elucidate the broad spectrum of responsibilities which we are now coming to realize belong to physical education.

First of all, physical education is concerned with human movement. It is concerned with movement as an expression of systemic function, as a modality of human understanding and performance, as an agent in the education process. There are many facets of education which are interested in specific aspects of movement, but physical education concerns itself with all human movement; through the study of such mobility it seeks to appreciate, understand, predict, and control the life design.

Secondly, physical education is concerned with functional integrity, a fitness of the individual that will permit and enhance movement. This functional integrity is fostered through tasks that involve strength, agility, flexibility, endurance, and coordination. It is a fitness which is concerned with the whole person, recognizing that every functional order of the human being affects all other functions. Integrity is not just biological, it is social and psychic as well. However, by and large, the biological base of functional integrity might well be considered the *sine qua non* of man's ability.

Thirdly, physical education is interested in play. Play is one of man's great cultural developments, and it may well be the basic mode of cultural transmission. Play is found in the opportunity to test oneself against unknown odds in a game situation which resembles lifelike reality. Play is imitation of societal activities, set within a prescribed area and a fixed time. Play is important to human understanding for it encompasses the multiple aspects of socialized, educated, and physically educated man.

STUDY OF MAN

Alexander Pope asserted that "the proper study of mankind is man," and thus it is to man that we must turn for understanding. Acknowledging that the arts, the humanities, and philosophy all have a contribution to make in the study of man, it is to the sciences that we will look to ascertain the social structure of man. The biological and physical sciences attempt to describe the structure of man and his universe, while the behavioral sciences study how man acts within his physical context.

Human individuality is based upon gross physical characteristics, superficial characteristics, physiological expression, sensations—including drives and reflexes—and cephalic patterning. Man as an individual and as part of a group is always at the beck and call of his natural or geographic environment, his heredity, and the cultural atmosphere created by his forebears. In order to go beyond these limitations, the behavioral sciences, as they attempt to understand man, seek objectivity of observation, relative concern for all men, ethnic neutrality, a discernment of simplicity which fosters parsimony, and finally skepticism about all findings.

Traditionally psychology has been interested in individual behavior. Anthropology is interested in the study of man, physical and cultural. Sociology is interested in the study of human relations and interactions, and physical education is interested in mobile man as he functions in play.

Each of these separate disciplines is interrelated with the others, and it is difficult to draw a firm line to isolate any one from another. However, we shall attempt to look at the social behavior of man through the sciences of sociology and anthropology and to find therein understandings about man's mobility.

science of social behavior

Until the time of Auguste Comte (1798–1857) there was no real understanding of the group as an entity with a personality and structure all its own. It had been assumed that individuals made up groups and that group behavior was a collection of the composite behavior of many people. Comte identified the group as a separate entity with a character unique to its structure, and thus was born the science of social statistics and dynamics. Comte believed that society was evolving toward perfection and that the evolutionary process would take time and could not be hurried to any great degree.

Herbert Spencer (1820–1903) further identified group composition, bringing to light information relative to the family, politics, and religion. In suggesting that social control was related to industry and work, Spencer's contributions to the science of human behavior supported the concept of the interaction of groups and the resulting controlled behavior.

Emile Durkheim (1858–1917), a man who gave direction to the understanding of social behavior, elucidated the concept of the science of societies and the results of interaction. He believed that society was governed by universal laws and constructs and that once these were identified it would be possible to predict social behavior and ultimately to control it.

Max Weber (1864–1920) suggested that sociology was a science which should attempt to interpret the understandings of social action so that the scientist could arrive at a causal explanation of the course and events peculiar to human social behavior.

Today both sociology and social anthropology study social institutions and their interactions. The social group is the unit of observation, and behavioral systems are observed and defined. These behavioral systems are composed of social norms which have a role-playing requirement. The norms are attached to positions and the positions demand role performance and hence social acts. The organization and disorganization of the behavioral systems of the social group thus are studied.

The sciences of social behavior are interested in personality, society, culture, human groups, social stratification, social change, and primary and secondary institutions and groups.

According to Inkeles, the models which are used in the study of sociology are evolutionary, organismic, balanced, and statistical-mathematical (1964). The evolutionary model assumes that society is evolving, supposedly in the direction of perfection; the organismic model is based on a structural-functional continuum; the balanced model looks at society with regard to equilibrium and conflict; and the statistical and mathematical model makes analogies according to sociometric reasoning and probability inference.

The difficulties of all of the sciences of social behavior lie in the nature and complexity of the material. Man is the subject of study, and man related to man is a very difficult concept to identify. Any study of human behavior and performance has difficulty with the control of experimentation. Unfortunately men do not arrange themselves as carefully as laboratory mice or green beans, for the study of man is the study of the organism which is subject to the greatest amount of variability. There are times when psychology can retreat to animal experimentation and draw inferences for man, but sociology and social anthropology can never do this with any degree of reality. Man's social groups are unlike those of any other animal. Finally, the study of man, by man, always must be cognizant of the vested interests of the scientist.

The study of behavior is difficult because any prediction about it may alter it. The group almost always is shifting and ambiguous, and this lack of stability confounds the picture. In addition to the aforementioned problems in the study of social behavior, the logical complexities of interaction are always present. For example, the structure and behavior of a football team is considerably different when they are "working out" in a scrimmage than when they are playing a game against an archrival. In the latter situation, the social group involves the opponents as well as the team, and the complexities of interaction between these two groups may make the picture nebulous and obscure.

METHODOLOGY IN THE STUDY OF MAN

Man has always sought to find the "truth" and has subscribed to many methods in the discovery process. First of all, he usually employs empirical reasoning. Here he observes what seems to be and concludes that what seems to be, is; therefore, it must be true. A certain amount of faith must be present in empirical judgments, for too much doubt or skepticism will destroy the truth factor. We apply value judgments to events, we ascertain results, and we draw the "truth" from observations of independent variables.

Secondly, in his search for truth man may use prophetic judgment. Here he asks the prophet what is the truth and accepts his judgment. In this sense, truth is ascertained when a prophet, who has supplied the right credentials of his wisdom, announces that truth has been exposed.

Thirdly, man may employ speculation in his search for truth. Speculation is usually based upon either prophetic judgment or empirical observations, and "truth" is discerned in what "ought to be."

Fourthly, man may utilize logic in his quest for truth. He sets up major and minor premises and deduces from these premises certain obvious inferences. This is known as *a priori* reasoning and has a certain presumptive flavor. On the other hand, man may employ the logic of induction and move from the part to the whole, from particulars to generals, from the individual to the universal. This is known as *a posteriori* reasoning and tends to have a synthetic flavor.

The fifth way in which man searches for truth, and the most exacting, is by means of the scientific method. Science is interested in the organization of men and materials; it insists upon an objective attitude, a method for analyzing facts, a set of generalized conclusions, and a coherent body of theoretical generalizations which hopefully will comprise theory. The steps of the scientific method are exacting and lucid. There can be no deviation from the scheme. The requirements of scientific inquiry must be met.

The scientific method always is organized along the following steps in the order noted:

DEFINITION OF THE PROBLEM AND FORMULATION OF A HYPOTHESIS. A problem is usually identified through observation and interest, and a hypothesis (a tentative assumption) is drawn up with regard to the problem. Hence, one might have observed that many boys who have athletic ability tend to be popular. The formulation of the hypothesis might suggest that "Boys who have a high degree of motor ability also have a high degree of social acceptability."

TESTING OF THE HYPOTHESIS THROUGH OBSERVATION AND ANALYSIS. An experimental design should be constructed to test the hypothesis, using the most critical and reliable instruments available. Hence, one might select a sample of young men who had a high degree of motor ability, as measured by one of the standardized motor ability tests, and another sample of young men who had a low degree of motor ability as measured by the identical test. Then to both of these groups one would administer a test which purported to measure social acceptance. One would analyze the data obtained (in this case through statistical methods) to find evidence for either accepting or rejecting the hypothesis at a certain level of statistical confidence.

STATEMENT OF THE CONCLUSION. The conclusion is stated from the facts at hand, and anything which does not have supportive evidence must not be suggested. Hence, one might conclude from the above data—as several researchers in this area of concern have concluded—that, from the samples drawn, there appears to be a high correlation between motor ability and social acceptability. The hypothesis would be found tenable. It is important to note that the restrictions and limitations of the conclusion are found in the sample, the data-gathering instruments, and the influence of chance. But even with all of those restrictions, a facet of knowledge is elucidated, with evidence, and we are closer to the truth than we were before the experiment.

PREDICTION OF THEORY. The researcher utilizing the scientific method is expected to be able to predict generalized theory with regard to his conclusions. Admittedly, such a theory is only an educated guess, but upon such educated guesses truth is established. Hence, one might suggest from the aforementioned experiment that the ability to move with facility is a premium quality in our society, and that social acceptance recognizes this attribute. One might even go a step further and predict that athletics and social acceptance are related. Such generalized theory might lead to further experimentation in the field of athletic prowess and societal approval and to an interest in ascertaining the relationship between societal status and athletic ability.

Theory with regard to social behavior may be either substantive or methodological, to use Gittler's terms (1957). Substantive theory is the "what" of social understanding and is comprised of concepts and propositions about social reality. Methodological theory deals with the "how" of social behavior and is concerned with the *modus operandi* of sociological inquiry.

VERIFICATION OF THE TRUTH. This final stage of the scientific method involves replication of the experiment by other scientists. If a hypothesis is really tenable, any other scientist drawing a like sample, utilizing the same data-gathering techniques, and employing the same analytical treatment of the facts would have to come to the identical conclusion, within the limits of chance probability. Replication is the hallmark of science. It is the final and most exacting test, and a real scientist would not consider that the truth had been exposed unless there had been substantial replication. Science is dynamic and self-correcting, and verification is the *sine qua non* of the scientific method.

It should be emphasized that the scientific method, while logical, organized, and lucid, does not always have all of the answers. Science threatens to become a myth of our time, and we must recognize the limitations of the method as well as its potentialities. There are some things that are difficult to assess quantitatively and are not subject to scientific methodology. It is difficult to measure degrees of love and hate; it is hard to gauge strength of interrelationships; it is not easy to quantify motives and intentions.

Because of these difficulties, the social scientist sometimes must utilize other than scientific means of inquiry. One of the controversial ways that this is done is through the concept of *verstehen.*

Verstehen, which is the German word meaning *to understand,* seeks to explain human social action through a scheme of intuitive understanding and guessed meaning. This technique provides the opportunity to explore "hunches" suggested by experts. Techniques based on *verstehen* recognize the uniqueness of human social behavior and acknowledge that it is subject to analysis through science and study, even if the specific techniques utilized must vary from those used by the natural sciences. The principle of *verstehen* often suggests the framework of an operational theory and then encourages and abets the scientific method in verifying or rejecting the theory.

The methodology used in the study of man is diverse and prolific, but each method helps to acquire, order, and interpret man's knowledge and thus to augment the understanding of human behavior.

IMPLICATIONS FOR PHYSICAL EDUCATION

Since physical education is interested in man and his movement behavior, it is imperative that physical educators understand the social context of man. Man can never be viewed as a simple biological organism. Man is not a machine, and the mechanistic theory of man cannot be accepted by physical education. Man cannot be viewed as a behavioral entity with no human relations and no societal direction. Man does not react to stimuli as a lone energy system, and human theory cannot be based entirely upon a stimulus-response bond. Man must be acknowledged as a social being—a creator and recipient of his cultural milieu. He always reacts in relation to his societal references, and he is never completely objective about his world.

Physical education is interested in socialized, educated man as approached through movement-oriented behavior. Physical education, because it is fascinated with "whole man," tends to utilize the arts, the humanities, and the physical, biological, and social sciences in its understandings. However, movement, play, and fitness have strong behavioral implications, and so we must turn to the behavioral sciences to gather facets of truth which will reveal the design of total man.

The pattern of moving to learn as we learn to move promises to become increasingly more important in understanding the design of man.

II

Man's Cultural Heritage

"Hey, that's not fair"

Intrinsic to man's social behavior are the rules and boundaries which determine his actions. Man never acts as an isolated biological organism; he always acts in terms of his cultural interpretation of himself and his society. Thus, when the adolescent complains that something is "not fair," he is making a judgment relative to the social behavior which is a part of the cultural atmosphere in which he lives. What isn't fair in one society may be perfectly acceptable in another, and what may not be fair for one age group can be a preferred pattern of behavior for a different age group. It isn't fair for the teen-aged boy to snatch the ball from his little sister, but it is quite understandable if baby brother grabs the ball from big sister. Baby brother has not been socialized sufficiently to understand the culturally oriented patterns existing between youth and age, male and female. It isn't fair for the high school football player publicly to berate his opponent, yet the sandlot player is allowed to tell his opponent that "you cheated." Our cultural heritage determines where and when specific behavior has social approval.

Man alone has the ability to create and transmit his social environment, and his culture consists of all the interactions between all men in adapting to that environment. Thus, culture will include all of the material and immaterial creations of man that are transmitted from generation to generation with what modifications any single era makes in those creations.

As defined by E. B. Tyler, "Culture is that complex whole which includes knowledge, belief, art, morals, law, custom, and any other capabilities acquired by man as a member of society" (1924, p. 1). Carleton Coon has more recently defined culture as "the sum total of the ways in which human beings live, transmitted from generation to generation by learning" (1954, p. 5). It is apparent that culture is not only the heritage of man, but also the means by which human behavior is regulated by the members of a particular society.

The humanist has a tendency to cull man's activities, interests, and products, and to designate them as cultural, but the sociologist and social anthropologist defines culture as the entire social heritage and history of man. The culture concept is the very foundation of the social sciences, providing a permanance and stability which gives meaning to behavior. Man is the product of his past as well as the builder of his present.

Culture, a category and a tool, is acquired by all men, shared and transmitted as a value of society, and concerned with symbolic and meaningful systems and roles. The cultural heritage tends to gratify human needs and to help with the integration of diverse behavioral patterns into meaningful designs of purpose and intent.

As man recognizes and is aware of his cultural affiliation, he adjusts and adapts his environment, his organism, and the interplay between self and environment. Thus, when the cry is heard, "Hey, that's not fair," something has to happen! Either the behavior will persist and the consequences will be assumed, or the behavior will be altered.

It is not possible for man to be cultureless, for every reaction that he makes either fortifies and enhances the cultural pattern or negates and alters it. In moving from one culture to another, men tend to carry their cultural interpretations of behavior with them. Thus, it is difficult to accept regional and national cultural directives which differ significantly from the ones that are already a part of one's life pattern. It is even difficult to understand cultural differences from one situation to another, even when the situations are in the same societal structure. For example, men find it hard to understand why one does not cheer in a women's game of field hockey, and women cannot comprehend how it is possible to deride the baseball umpire and still accept his decisions.

CULTURAL ACQUISITIONS

Ruth Benedict has noted that "the cultural pattern of any civilization makes use of a certain segment of the great arc of potential human purposes and motivations" (1924, p. 219). Culture is built around the basic problems and responsibilities that man faces as a part of his societal membership.

individual problems

Man's individual problems are many and varied. He must be concerned with rearing the young and providing food and shelter for himself and those for whom he is responsible. The ways in which these necessities are handled have certain cultural implications. For example, the young are not raised, ordinarily, by a party outside the home, for their social education is the home's responsibility; food and shelter are obtained through acceptable methods, and the rights of others are respected.

Man needs communication with other men, and he invents language and movement symbols to convey meaning and purpose. The members of any single society recognize the language and symbols of their culture, even though that communication is incomprehensible to others.

Organization and social control are also important human problems. The complexity of society makes it necessary that there be some specialization of work and role, and that this division of labor be organized in such a way that it has meaning to the individual. The way in which the societal organization is structured, the controls that are built into that organization, and the individual's understanding of the pattern of specialization make up a large part of the cultural heritage.

Humans also have problems with regard to their relations with outsiders, those persons who fall outside the societal boundaries. The cultural mode of behavior gives direction as to the acceptance or rejection of strangers.

Another of man's problems deals with his relationship with the supernatural. Cultural directives suggest appropriate attitudes and concepts; for example, the supernatural may be feared and held in awe, or it may be revered and turned to for comfort and security.

Man also seeks the meaning and motivation for his life, attempting to understand the meaning of his environment and his relationship to it. Such understanding borders on the metaphysical, yet it is a necessity in man's individual acquisition of his cultural perspective.

Cultural dispositions are transmitted to the child in a very personalized way by those responsible for his rearing. The child acquires the culture through frustrations and identifications. He is told "No, no" to all things not approved or not a part of the culture, and is told "Good boy" with regard to those patterns which are acceptable.

societal problems

The responsibility of the total group for its culture differs from that of the individual. The society acknowledges that culture is learned and seeks to set up institutions whereby the learning can be facilitated. The church, the school, the home are all such basic primary institutions which play a part, in some form, in most societies.

Since societal culture is derived from environmental, biological, psychological, and historical components, it is imperative that culture be structured in such a way that the various integral parts are readily apparent to the individual. This structure need not always be formal, but it must be discernible.

Any cultural pattern is both dynamic and variable. There are basic cultural components which remain fixed in spite of the fact that culture is in a state of constant flux. It is an instrument of adjustment for society and it gives means for the creative expression.

However, in spite of its dynamic and changing aspects, the societal culture does exhibit regularities which permit and encourage analysis. Thus, in the United States, where the Judeo-Christian ethic provides the norms for behavior, the culture reflects such an ethic, making prediction and analysis possible. The Judeo-Christian ethic suggests the value of individual life, and we might expect to see this concept reflected in the cultural understandings of America; we would expect the individual to be granted opportunities for development of self in many situations. Such an expectation provides the first step in the analysis of physical education and the prediction of its future direction.

Cultural imperatives push society toward conformity; thus Cuber has observed that there is a constant "strain toward consistency" (1947). Because society acknowledges that the behavior of peoples is a learned process, an effort is made to see that the cultural heritage of the society becomes the fundamental reason behind behavior. If society accepts the concept of competition as a part of its cultural pattern, there will always be forms of competition available in most aspects of human life. We might reason, therefore, that structured competition in the athletic world is a cultural imperative and not just the enthusiastic whim of an individual or a small committee.

CULTURAL ORGANIZATION

The organization of the culture is usually structured in discernible patterns. These patterns result from the obligation to teach other people the cultural heritage. Thus, social institutions have specific responsibilities and a specific identity; when there is some interchange of responsibilities between two social institutions, there is usually controversy. The controversy generated by the Supreme Court's decision to ban prayer in public education is one example of the problems caused by institutional interresponsibility. Another example can be seen in the "big-time" athletic structure in the universities of the country. The economic order has limits that are not supposed to infringe upon the educational order and when they do, there is controversy.

Society recognizes that its cultural heritage exists in both material and immaterial form. The huge football stadiums, the sprawling community schools, the team uniforms, and the box office are all material indicators of culture, but no less real are the concepts of challenging the umpire's authority, the pep talk, loyalty to school and team, and belief in athletic grants-in-aid.

A cultural heritage is uniformly shared by all members of a society and, although certain groups have certain prerogatives in behavior with regard to cutural standards, the standards, material artifacts, and nonmaterial concepts belong to each individual in the society equally. Thus, the casual spectator can be just as involved in cheering a college team to victory as the alumni and students of the participating college. People develop loyalties to cultural ideas and artifacts in independent ways which can result in identical behavior patterns.

Culture shapes the pattern of societal life, but, because of its continual fluctuation and change, it is difficult to isolate a stable and fixed cultural pattern. The individuals within the society can either conform or not conform to the pattern, for reasons best known to themselves, but they cannot deny their culture or ignore it.

Education, which has the responsibility of transmitting the cultural pattern, also makes use of the strength of a cultural identification and, although it seeks to *change* the pattern, it changes it only as it changes itself. Education, medicine, law, and some of their subdivisions cling tenaciously to old cultural traits which have long been defunct. This can be deleterious to progress, but at the same time it can insure some small degree of cultural security.

CULTURAL IDENTIFICATION

Obviously, the cultural pattern is always set in some type of natural environment, and it is just as apparent that the individuals of a society bring certain genetic dispositions to their societal identification. Even society itself has a type of genetic description. However, Ogburn and Nimkoff believe that "variations in natural environment and heredity do not contribute as much to the explanation of difference in man's social life as do the variations in the cultural environment" (1964, p. 27). Therefore, if we wish to understand man's behavior and his mobile symbols, it is necessary that we understand his cultural milieu. The smallest unit of a cultural system might be called a *culture trait*. When traits which are normally associated together are studied and analyzed, we are dealing with *trait complexes,* and when complexes which are related to each other are studied, we have a *culture pattern*. Cultural patterns formulate the culture of a given society.

Any given culture will select and borrow traits from adjacent cultures and will invent new traits and discard old ones. Cultural patterns for any specific society vary, and this variation is determined by such things as the physical and biological environment of a society, its geographic isolation, internal elaboration, technological position, and dominant themes, especially as these are colored by ethnocentrism (the belief that one's culture is superior to all others).

Athletic events, sports, and meaningful human mobility are cultural traits in almost all societies. Dances, games, movement symbols, and mobile interaction are cultural universals and should be studied as a possible clue to society's structure.

Linton suggests that *cultural universals* are those elements in any society which all adults acquire as a matter of course—things like language, dress, housing, and moral values (1936, Chap. 6). He identified *cultural specialities* as those elements which were shared only by certain groups within the society. Thus, cultural specialities might be occupational, sexual, or regional in nature. Finally, Linton suggested that *cultural alternatives* are different techniques for attaining the same goal in society. The massing of an economic fortune might involve several permissible and sanctioned cultural alternatives.

In the cultural pattern of the United States, it can be assumed that athletics are structured so as to encourage certain moral values and this structure can be construed as a *cultural universal*. The *cultural specialty* within the athletic world might be concerned with the different patterns suggested for men and women athletes. Men are encouraged and permitted to engage in team sports on a professional level with monetary rewards. Women, on the other hand, are expected to participate in team sports only on an amateur basis, with female professionalism allowed only in activities which are individual or dual. The *cultural alternatives* are found in the way in which championships are recognized. The patterns are diverse; amateur and professional, male and female, school and community, national and international; but the championship concept is recognized as essential, and alternatives are permitted.

Culture is probably the only uniform source of human behavior, for it provides the outline of appropriate responses to the needs of the interacting members of the group. Although a culture provides the norms, beliefs, and values for any group of people, it is not necessary for every norm to have a value. Mott suggests that the *prescribed norms* of a society are found in the "thou shalt" and the "thou shalt not" dictums; such norms obviously do have value (1965). Sociey also has *permissive norms* which allow but not require certain actions. There is also the *norm of preference* where certain actions are preferred but not required. To find illustrations of this in the terms of physical education, we might say that fair play and consideration for opponents are the prescribed norms of any game situation; that the drive to win at any cost short of cheating is permissible; and that the ability to accept loss or victory with philosophical tranquility is a preferred norm. Obviously, there are infractions and disregard for the norms on many occasions, but when they occur, it is not with cultural endorsement.

A group attempts, by the use of *sanctions* and *roles,* to convince individuals within the society that they must conform to the culture. A sanction is a reward for adhering to the cultural directive, or a punishment for violating a prescribed norm. A role imposes an obligation which is usually enforced by means of status acknowledgement or its lack. Hence, the "good guy" is allowed to wear a white hat and marry the girl in our western stories, and the superior athlete wins the Olympic gold medal and becomes the hometown hero. The role of the athlete usually carries with it a value connotation of "good" and has an aura of such concepts as fair, understanding, humble, and heroic, which are positive status-building symbols.

Cultural identification happens in a society when the culture gratifies the needs of any specific group and when the identification pattern can be integrated into the societal pattern of values and beliefs. Thus, we might say that culture creates and sanctions itself, it directs its own change, and it gives values to its innovations and design.

Communication is a very important part of cultural identification, and there are many sociologists and anthropologists who believe that human language is the *sine qua non* of human society. This may well be, if we will consider language as including more than spoken and written words. Human movement patterns have been a basic part of the communication of all people at all levels in all societies. This movement language is a continuum including certain unstructured features found in gestures and certain structured and styled features found in the art form of dance. There is no reason to believe that the specific symbolism of any one society is understood in all societies, but there is reason to believe that some form of human movement is utilized as expression in all known societies. Patterns of human movement might come as close to being a universal trait of all groups as language itself—for indeed, movement is the special hallmark of the conative domain which identifies human understandings.

CULTURAL DESCRIPTION

The role that an individual is expected to play within a society is strongly influenced by certain cultural categories which have been identified as folkways, mores, taboos, and laws. The *folkways* of a society are the expected ways of performance for all individuals and, although these can change, they tend to have both permanence and a rationale which is not always discernible. The *mores* are much stronger social rules than the folkways, and they support behavior which is crucial to identity and survival as far as the group is concerned. An ignored or violated folkway is tolerated, but the mores are societal expectations which are subject to sanction. *Taboos* are rules which indicate cultural wrongs, and taboos always carry value judgments. The *laws* are the planned rules of society and must receive some form of societal endorsement before they are adopted. Laws often grow out of folkways, mores, and taboos, but they can also be conceived with regard to the organization of the society and the transmission of its cultural heritage. Laws, by their very nature, are concerned with morality. They have a history and cultural atmosphere of their own, and although they reflect a society's culture, they also create it. Laws may be customary and lack codification, or they may be the enacted products of an organized civilization. Whether enacted or customary, they are usually regulatory and thus enforce the mores.

It stands to reason that if we can understand the mores, folkways, taboos, and laws of any society, we should be able to anticipate certain behavioral patterns and then provide the behavioral controls needed to augment the progress of social change. The regulations of a society help to maintain the discipline, and without discipline society is chaotic disorganization.

CULTURAL SIGNIFICANCE

If one wishes to understand the people within any society, it is necessary to examine the culture of that country. Cultural identification is difficult because it is always based on the subjective analysis of the observer, and when the observer is a product and transmitter of the culture himself, his identification of significant cultural trends is always circumspect. Nevertheless, in order to better understand the ideas which underlie movement behavior in the United States, it would be wise to see what the American cultural design seems to suggest.

Judeo-Christian ethic

America has been mainly a product of the tenets found within the Judeo-

Christian ethic. The spiritual interpretation of individual salvation has suggested the individual value of each person in the society. The reverence for human life, the direct communication with a deity, and trust, faith, and love with respect to an understanding but demanding god have all colored the American cultural pattern with a certain hue of individuality. This religious influence can be overtly witnessed on many occasions other than those institutionalized by the church. The belief that prayer is necessary in opening a large meeting or convention, the invocation asked on ceremonial occasions such as commencements and inaugurations, and the use of prayer before certain events which demand an all-out individual effort, such as an athletic contest, are mute testimonials of the sweeping effect of the Judeo-Christian ethic in American life.

casualness

There is a minimum of central authority in America, and, because of the democratic principles of self-determination, a casualness has resulted which can be found in both material and immaterial traits. The casualness of attire which allows a broad array of clothing to be worn on many occasions is one such material trait. The "patio-living" life which is identified with many sections of the country is yet another. There is a casualness of behavior found in the use of the terms of address, and there is a casualness of practice with regard to social custom and the tenets of etiquette. Because of this casualness, there is an easy tolerance for differences within the society. The observation that "it's not hurting anyone, so let him alone," is a favorite expression of this tolerance on the part of Americans. Many of the ceremonies of life have been permitted to assume a casual aura, and the bizarre arrangements for some funerals and marriages are expressions of this. In sport and games, casualness depends on the degree of difficulty and perfection. There is a great casualness about the "pick-up" game, the friendly golf match, the neighborhood tennis game; but there is much less casualness with regard to professional games, where the rules "count" because the score depends upon them.

goodness of man

Americans tend to believe in the goodness of man. They do not subscribe to the concept that man is born wicked into a good world and that in order to attain salvation he must be made good. Instead, we subscribe to the belief that man is born good into an evil world and that he must spend a great part of his life resisting the temptations and evil customs that the world fosters. The goodness of man suggests that all human beings in the American society generally are accepted for what they are, and they seldom must present credentials of birth, status, or even economic position to participate in a plan of action. Thus, every child has the potentiality to be what he wants and there is the very real belief that any baby can grow up to be President. Sports always proceed under the basic assumption that the opponents are "good" as far as intent and integrity are concerned and that the best man will win. Of course, this is the cultural ideal and is not always realized in practice. There are times when individuals or systems may reject the cultural pattern for what seems to be good reason based upon experience. However, for the most part, when you agree to play against another in a game situation, you are assuming that your opponent is "good" in a moral and ethical way and that all people and situations are equal.

personal mobility

In American culture it is generally understood that each man has mobility within the society. Based upon many factors of cultural perception, this belief has been the bedrock of American life. Man is allowed to have *horizontal mobility* with no questions asked. That is, he is allowed to move in any area within one social stratum with a minimum amount of societal wonder or condemnation and usually total acceptance of his decisions. The American can move from job to job, from neighborhood to neighborhood, from team to team, and there is no judgment that this mobility is not desirable or not expected. In addition, the American is allowed *vertical mobility,* which permits him to move up and down from one stratum to another. It is the "right" of the American to make himself "better" than his father. Most parents desire for their children a position with regard to finances, education, property ownership, and status which can be interpreted as better than they had for themselves. The American child is taught early that he can make of himself whatever he wishes, and there are few barriers which are put in the way to deter him. There is even reason to suggest that the person who does not utilize the concept of vertical mobility is lazy, uncaring, and lacking ambition.

mastery of environment

Americans refuse to allow themselves to be mastered by their environment, and they seek continually to change the environment so that it conforms to the dictates of the individual's nature. Weather is predicted and may some day be controlled. Adaptation is made to the climate in terms of housing and clothing. The sea is "conquered" in our attempts to remove the salt, prevent erosion, seed the fishing grounds, and change tidal patterns. The air is "conquered" as we learn to utilize its characteristics for better flight patterns, to make more effective use of prevailing winds and jet streams, and to chart lows and highs, fronts and troughs. The American believes that he can adapt, adjust, and reconcile his natural environment and that he can ultimately predict and control that environment.

technological devotion

There is a fascination with technology in the United States which has produced technical improvements so rapidly that they have almost outdistanced cultural adaptations. The development of the motor to propel automobiles, airplanes, trains, and ships has been an American contribution to the technical development of the world. The "computerized society" which is developing, almost too rapidly, attests to American technological devotion. The belief is widespread that a machine will do a better job than a man, at less energy cost and with greater efficiency. We use machines to measure, to categorize, to work for our society, and our faith in the technology that we have developed is a powerful cultural pattern.

equality on an unequal basis

The American is philosophically convinced that "all men are created equal," but he tends to think that this creation is subject to uneven and unequal circumstances, so that there are some people who "are more equal than others." The inequality of man usually is thought to depend upon economic circumstances, racial affiliations, and sex. The legal directives of the American culture have attempted to make sure that the inequalities are minimized, but the social directives acknowledge the inequality and tend to maximize it in terms of status roles and societal expectations. The dramatic social revolution that is going on with respect to the civil rights of Negroes, the persistent evolution for social equality for women, and the controls being used to prevent financial domination of management are all examples of legal-social commitments of the culture to the equality of its members. We cannot expect the realization of a philosophical principle too rapidly, and it will probably be a long time until the unequal basis of equality is eliminated, if, indeed, it ever is.

pragmatic dedication

American society subscribes to a "what's-it-good-for" justification of everything that it does, and unless the answer to that very pertinent question comes forth immediately, an idea is usually discarded. Functionalism has placed its stamp on our cultural heritage. Educationally, the subjects and disciplines that have some "use" are the ones which tend to dominate the picture. The classics, art, higher mathematics, philosophy all must struggle to retain their tenuous hold on the school curriculum, and some have already lost what grip they had. Thus, if we cannot decide on its worth, any material or immaterial trait will be rejected by the American. In seeking to justify the worth of games, fitness, play, and meaningful movement to the society, physical education personnel have always couched their justification in terms of pragmatic interpretations. We play games because they teach people about life; we advocate fitness for health, survival, and physiological efficiency; we move to learn. These explanations are usually acceptable because they reflect pragmatic dedication. There seems to be evidence that this dedication is intensifying rather than abating, and it promises to retain and enlarge its importance.

aggressive competence

The American places a premium upon certain personality attributes, and both aggression and competence are high on this list. The two-fisted, hard-hitting fighter who conquered the west; the self-made, forceful, able man who dominates the business world; the powerful, decisive, capable athlete who guides his team to victory or who masters his weak, vacillating, inept opponent are all idealized pictures of "red-blooded Americans." It is interesting to note that although we value this personality trait in the cultural pattern, we tend to give it a sexual identification. It is not appropriate for a woman to possess aggressive competence, as it is for a man. Culturally, we like to believe that our women are more submissive and less able. However, there is room for admiration for the woman who can rise to the occasion of leadership, who has the ability to display aggressive competence, although we like to see her do it in what is thought of as a "feminine way." Obviously such ambivalence in cultural expectations can provide many reasons for a social dilemma, especially in sex role playing. This is brought into view forcefully in terms of the woman athlete who must display aggression in order to win, who must be competent in order to be victorious, and yet who, at the same time, must be "womanly." A great deal of the difficulty that the American woman has had in discerning her sex-oriented role stems from the fact that the cultural concept of the female role negates the cultural concept of the American personality.

collective conformity

The American enjoys groups. He likes group membership and identification and he seeks to conform to group standards. Even in his rebellion against societal standards, he seeks a group to which to belong, and adopts the conformity pattern of that group. There is an obvious "sameness" about most of the social deviates. The cut of the hair, the type of clothing, the kind of music they like, the sort of art which has appeal, all have identifiable characteristics, and the deviate emerges as the "beatnik," the social reformer, the "hippie," the "far out man." The desire for conformity and collectivism can be found in less extreme forms within America. The subcultural identification of the teen-ager is one such example. The adolescent seeks identification with his kind, and he will conform to the pattern set by the subculture, so that even our subcultures exhibit a type of collective behavior which is readily identified by the majority of the society. The athlete very often displays a collective conformity which is his hallmark. He wears an identifying emblem such as a school letter, he tends to adopt certain clothes patterns and styles, and he enjoys his collective association with his fellow athletes.

youth-directed

The cult of the young seems to be an integral part of the American cultural heritage, manifesting itself in a fascination with youth seldom seen in other cultures. The American woman seeks to retain her youth as symbolized by body type, clothes, and attitude; and she accomplishes this with the aid of cosmetics, dieting, exercise, and judicious clothing choices. Her male counterpart is just as concerned, and he uses as aids for youth retention the toupee, the clean-shaven face, the "ivy league look," and intensive workouts for figure control. There is an American dread of growing old and a concomitant desire to "think young" and belong to the younger generation. This cultural adherence to youth makes the tolerance of a youth-centered society much more acceptable, and there are indications that we have allowed the adolescent subculture to dominate the societal scheme of America.

future orientation

There is the strong and cherished belief in America that no matter how bad today has been, surely "tomorrow will be better." Americans look toward each new tomorrow with hope and faith. The American commitment to the perfectability of man, the improvement of society, and the increase in the material comforts of the future all make the orientation to tomorrow a part of "the great American dream." If you lose the game today, there is "always another day."

CULTURAL TRANSMISSION

Although society has certain specific institutions to transmit the culture, it is evident that cultural spread is dependent upon more than the formalized educational system. The culture tends to diffuse in a number of different ways. Diffusion, which is the mobility of a cultural trait or complex from its central origin, can be either purposeful or nonpurposeful. Purposeful diffusion includes the school system and less formalized structures such as missionary work. Purposeful cultural diffusion is found in the work of the Peace Corps, the Job Corps, Operation Headstart, and many other federal programs. Nonpurposeful diffusion occurs as members of the society interact with other people in a different societal structure. Thus, the American tourist and American movies and television have had a tremendous impact on other societies and have diffused the American cultural pattern throughout the world. Many societies have criticized the United States sharply for this diffusion and have not looked kindly upon the assimilation of new cultural perspectives within their own societal patterns.

The diffusion of the culture seems to depend upon the idea that it has an appeal for other people. It has been noted by Landis that the appeal for diffusion usually is made in practical, sensory, intellectual terms (1958). The technological devotion of the American culture certainly has had a practical appeal to other societies. The personal mobility pattern has a certain sensory appeal, as do many of the material traits of American-made articles and American foods. The concept of equality and the orientation to the future both have intellectual appeal and might be adopted readily by those societies whose culture permits a fascination with such concepts.

There is a time when cultural diffusion can reach the point of saturation, so that a society will rebel against the presence of any aspects of a foreign culture being allowed to infringe upon the existing cultural pattern. In the past, Japan protected herself by closing the doors to all alien ideas and people. France rebelled by insisting that American airfields be closed, and there has been a general wave of protest against American cultural diffusion, with the slogan "Yankee, go home" plastered on many buildings.

Cultural inertia is the reluctance of a society to accept change as a part of its pattern. Traditionally, the rural people in the United States have been loath to accept cultural change. Certain professional groups seem possessed of a cultural inertia which resists change, and in the athletic world we often see a cultural inertia which can be most frustrating.

A *cultural lag* occurs when one aspect of a culture persists beyond its period of usefulness, falling behind other elements in the culture with which it was previously associated. Thus, there has been a cultural lag with regard to the use of alcohol in the American society. A society which frowns on alcohol but nevertheless allows a youth-centered culture to have permissive behavioral standards cannot expect societal comprehension, let alone social endorsement. Legal restriction becomes a cultural lag. There are many more subtle cultural lags. The adoration of the "strong man" is not feasible in a society which has used technology to master all situations involving strength, which has walked in space, and which has seen power result from electricity instead of muscle fiber.

Cultural transmission, both within and without the society, is the process which connects past with future. It is not only the culture itself, but its form of transmission which is the gigantic molding mechanism for human personality. Cultural identifications and an understanding of cultural transmission often creates marginal men—men who span two societies with different cultural traits.

CULTURAL CONTRIBUTIONS

Culture gives to society a character, an identification matrix, a past, and a future. The patterns of the culture depend upon physical, verbal, and material behavior of the society. In coping with human problems, human societies· must choose from a limited number of solutions within the cultural milieu. Such choice involves a value operation based on concepts of desirability. From these choices there is the possibility of societal invention which can remake the cultural heritage. This invention is usually an accumulative process rather than an individual act, and is only permissible because cultural directives make it possible. As values are formed, social norms accrue, and from these come behavioral standards and societal discipline. Adjustment to the discipline will depend upon the "goodness of the fit" and the balance of the parts. A society can never be without a culture, and culture must always have a societal basis. These are interdependent, symbiotic entities.

IMPLICATIONS FOR PHYSICAL EDUCATION

The scope, the past and future directions of physical education are dependent upon the cultural pattern of the society of which it is a part. The place of games and sports in American society is a fairly well established cultural trait, and thus games have the opportunity to mold the cultural heritage as well as be molded by it. Movement is itself one of the significant communication symbols of our culture and can lend tremendous influence to cultural transmission. The attitude of the individual toward the concepts of play, fitness, and movement will be governed by the cultural identification attached to those concepts. It is possible that the athlete forms a subculture of his own, and thus the adolescent athlete is subject to the tenets from at least two subcultures which have certain divergent points of view. Physical education has a very real responsibility to enrich the cultural heritage, to provide innovative techniques for cultural change, and to assist with cultural transmission.

Man's Cultural
Potential

"What 'chu wanna be?"

One of the most nebulous aspects of man is his personality structure. We are not born with personalities, although there may be certain hereditary dispositions toward specific attributes. It takes the environment to shape personality, and man is continually molded by his physical and cultural environment. Personality is amorphous and resists stabilization. There is never any one time in your life when you can say, "this is my personality," for tomorrow many things may have changed. Man's personality is strongly influenced by his interaction with other men, and this interaction is called socialization. The individual human nature which results from the socialization process is called personality.

SOCIALIZATION

In developing their personalities, human beings incorporate their culture within themselves. One's position in society involves an organized, individual pattern of feelings, actions, and thoughts, and one's concept of self reflects this pattern. Man carries his society around in his being.

Green has suggested that "selfhood arises from a person's awareness of what he shares with, and how he differs from, other persons through the adoption of their attitudes toward himself" (1956, p. 122). Thus, socialization is always a shared process in spite of the fact that any analysis of socialization must depend on introspection.

There is considerable disagreement regarding the influence of environment on heredity, but there is general consensus that environment provides opportunities for the unfolding of innate potentialities. In support of this construct there are numerous cases cited of supposedly feral children who grew up in an environment which was not human-oriented. These children ostensibly have followed the environmental pattern of their animal foster parents, and the literature is resplendent with stores of wild children and Tarzan-like men. However, it should be noted that there has been only sketchy documentation of these cases, and no authentic cases have been reported with scientific exactitude. It has never been ascertained that there were witnesses to the fact that children lived as a part of an animal group. Lately, some sociologists have suggested that there may be reason to suspect that the cases of the feral children are, in reality, cases of children who have mental limitations and who have been neglected.

Regardless of the disagreement about feral children, there is ample evidence to support the concept that cultural and physical environments do shape the person within the limits of heredity. The personality structure used within the roles which an individual plays changes according to the environmental situation. We are influenced by each situation which we meet.

development of self

Awareness of the self is sharpened by increased social differentiation and by conflict with others. Therefore, we might surmise that the self can be antisocial as well as social.

The individual uses other people as mirrors of his self, interpreting himself in the light of what he believes others think of him. Almost all humans need both conflictual and consensual validation of their impressions.

CONFLICTUAL VALIDATION. This is recognized when a self-assessment does not find verification through the interactions of others. Thus, you might think of yourself as an "understanding sportsman" and yet your colleagues suggest that you are ruthless, domineering, and aggressive on the athletic field. The typical tendency is to ignore the judgment of your colleagues if it does not coincide with your own analysis. However, when a large number of judgments in conflict with your own assessment are combined, they become increasingly difficult to ignore. Therefore, in the wake of such overwhelming opinion, you usually reassess your personality and emerge with an altered awareness of self.

CONSENSUAL VALIDATION. This occurs when there is a affiirmation of your own assessment of self through the actions and communications of others. Thus, if one regards himself as an "understanding sportsman," and if his friends and colleagues tend to suggest that he is thoughtful, self-effacing, and cooperative in game situations, then all of these traits will support the individual's assessment of self; this provides a consensus that he really is what he thought he was all along.

social judgment

An individual is not usually willing to accept the judgment of any one person as significant to his socialization, although every interaction leaves some trace. Perhaps the most important social judgments are those made by people with authority. Thus, the parents, the teacher, the doctor, the boss, the minister, the accepted leader will make judgments which carry a great deal of social weight for the individual. There is evidence to suggest that man only hears what he wants to hear, but it would appear that when the enunciation comes from authority, he tends to listen more closely.

Social judgments are also made by one's equals, and these judgments carry a special weight, particularly at certain ages. To the teen-ager, being subject to conflictual validation of social selfhood by people who are his equals can be traumatic. Thus, "what the boys think" becomes, to the adolescent, much more important than what Dad thinks, or what the teacher thinks. Judgments made by equals are always important, although adults tend more easily to ignore those judgments that are conflictual and to hear only those that are consensual. It is apparent that most people seek as friends those persons who will offer consensual validation of self-assessment. People who like you are your friends, and those who do not are not.

experiences

The development of the social self is influenced not only by judgment but also by experience. The habits and attitudes which are a part of sequential and repeated experiences make important contributions to the socialization process. Wishes—that is, internalized desires for specific experiences—also play a part. One may desire an experience in order to repeat a sensation one has already had, or one may desire an experience in the hope that it will prove to be a meaningful occasion to him in terms of his socialization.

Thus, if one has found excitement and meaning in a hotly contested tennis match, he may wish, at some later date, to reexperience those emotions in the same setting. Or after having watched others play on the varsity basketball team, one may long for the opportunity to have that experience oneself. When wishes materialize, they are not always what one imagined they would be, as most of us know, but an individual does not know for sure what the emotional commitment of an experience can be until his wish for it has been fulfilled.

Socialization may also come about as a result of a *unique experience,* encountered only once and without sequential possibilities. In one sense, all of life's experiences are unique, but either crisis or novelty tends to give the truly unique experience a sense of drama. Experiences involving death, marriage, or birth all tend to be unique; they are critical in the development of self and are not usually repeated. Experiences such as a parachute jump, an Olympic run, or a Rose Bowl game are novel and may be repeated, but often are not. The *unique experience* might be as inconsequential as a ride on the merry-go-round or the opportunity to play golf with a professional, but to the person involved, the experience has meaning and plays an important part in the socialization process.

Many social experiences are a part of group identification. The family and other primary groups often structure situations, purposefully, to make sure that individuals have the opportunity for life experiences. The group forces the individual to play a role that will offer a new participation experience and thus will assist or augment socialization. Fathers feel an obligation to take their sons to baseball games; mothers often feel that their daughters should be responsible for an important family occasion. Teachers place their students in positions of leadership, and ministers make a time and place for spiritual experiences which have unique implications.

It is not only the primary group which provides experiences for the individual. The *reference group* also has certain influences. The reference group is a group to which a person relates but to which he does not necessarily belong. Sometimes the reference group is a part of the wish syndrome of the individual. For example, a boy desiring very much to be a part of the scout movement will use that organization as his reference group and will attempt to pattern his habits and attitudes with regard to the scout group. The athletic team is a reference group for many people, and the behavior of the team is continually subject to a multitude of criticism. People feel keenly about athletic teams because they tend to identify themselves so completely with them. Therefore, when the athletic team does not live up to societal expectations many people are upset, for the team has been their reference group.

expectations

Just as an individual has his own personal expectations about attributes which he believes will result from the socialization process, so society has certain expectations about the results of the individual's socialization.

BASIC DISCIPLINE. Subjecting oneself to the aspirations and belief of society is a difficult task, but it is one of the expectations of the socialization process. There are times when the individual is expected to give up his self-determination for the welfare of the group; when individual interests conflict with group interests, if socialization has been effective, the individual recognizes the greater importance of group needs compared with his own. The quarterback will give the ball to someone else rather than attempt to run with it, because the team interest in obtaining a score is greater than his individual need to be the star. The center forward in hockey will "pass off" rather than attempt the drive herself, because the need of the team is greater than her own. This ability to subject individual desires to group need does not come easily to many people, and usually manifests itself only as the socialization process teaches a basic discipline. Socially structured behavior is demanding, but it is the hallmark of civilization.

ACCEPTED ASPIRATIONS. Society determines what are the accepted aspirations of the individuals who make up its structure. These aspiration determinations are products of the needs of the group as well as of the permissiveness of the group attitude. Thus, societal structure in the United States encourages the leadership role as an accepted aspiration for an individual, but the American cultural pattern dictates what sort of leadership can emerge and its limitations. A political dictator would not be tolerated; a monopolistic tycoon would not be tolerated; a "ball hog" is only partially tolerated. If the individual aspires to be something not accepted by society, he must either defy society or leave it. On the other hand, one must bear in mind that many of the innovations which have altered the cultural pattern, and hence the structure of society, have been initiated by those persons who dared to have aspirations that were not accepted by society. In such cases, through the tenacity and dedication of an individual, the expectations of society were changed.

NECESSARY SKILLS. The group expects that the socialization process will provide the necessary skills for the maintenance of the group, as well as the ways in which these skills may be acquired and practiced. As the society changes, many skill patterns are disregarded, and this always presents a problem. Technology has made certain labor skills useless, and large segments of the society are having to be resocialized with respect to the acquisition of certain skills. The automobile made the smithy's skills obsolete, just as Einstein's theory of relativity made obsolete some of the conventional weapons of warfare.

APPROPRIATE ROLES. The roles which the individual plays are always the choice of society. Even the role of societal antagonist is structured by the socialization process. Folkways, mores, taboos, and laws all govern individual roles, and while there is a certain amount of mobility permitted in any one role, the variety of roles is usually limited.

individual social evolution

The socialization process does not follow a random pattern, but tends to have certain identifiable stages. Piaget classified the child's socialization process into four distinct stages (1932). The first stage, he suggested, is one of "simple individual regularity," in which the child makes his own experiments with things, manipulating and structuring them to suit his own pleasures. This stage starts sometime after birth and continues until about the age of three. The rattle is banged against the crib, the blocks are thrown from the high chair, the teddy bear is squeezed and his ear pulled off, and big sister has her hair yanked by the baby.

The second stage suggested by Piaget is that of "egocentrism," a stage in which the child knows the rules but will adjust them for his own purposes, ignore them, or invent his own. In a sense, he is playing a game with himself —a game in which he is participant, umpire, and spectator. This stage usually occurs from the ages of about four to six. Thus, we note that during the egocentric stage the child will kick down the castle which has been constructed of blocks, will scream when he is put to bed although he knows that the rules say that he should be quiet and go to sleep, will refuse to eat his food because he doesn't like carrots, and will "tell on" his playmates to get his own way.

About the ages of seven through ten the child learns to obey the rules and to compete within the rule structure. Usually he simplifies the rules for the occasion and tends to invent rules which are in accord with his desires. For example, there is the case of the little girl who always won when she played solitaire. When questioned as to how this was possible, she said that she won by counting the number of "cheats" that she used. Thus, it was better to win with one cheat or no cheats than to win with ten cheats—but in any case she always won and she always followed the rules, including the "how-many-cheats" rule.

Sometime after the age of ten the majority of children make rules a part of their personality structure, internalizing those which make up the pattern suggested by the socialization process. If a rule is broken, they expect to be admonished according to the "rules of admonition." The young adolescent really expects to be reprimanded for disobeying his social conscience, and if that reprimand does not come, an alteration in behavior might well be expected. The first time the rule is not followed and he "gets by," he experiences guilt and apprehension, but the more the "get-by behavior" is repeated, the less is the fear of admonition or punishment and the easier it becomes to enact the same asocial behavior. It would seem, therefore, that we should see to it that important societal rules are enforced all of the time, and not just spasmodically. If respect for authority is of value in a society, then there must be instant admonition when such respect is not shown. The social deviate often has a pattern of defiance which starts quite early in life and which finally finds its expression in amoral or illegal behavior.

The evolutionary process of socialization proceeds at a different pace in all individuals. The pace is determined in part by environmental and hereditary factors and in part by the societal structure. Some societies, for example, deliberately keep their women at a slow pace of social evolution; some societies tend to slow down the pace of their children, recognizing and indulging childlike behavior on the part of mature individuals and thereby prolonging childhood into maturity.

societal influence

Individuals tend to be influenced through interaction and also through the total concept of the society itself. To the young woman who is about to gain American citizenship, the influence of American society has as great an impact as the interrelationships she may have had with individuals within the American society. "Being an American" means the recognition of a societal pattern, the understanding of a cultural heritage, and the awareness of societal influences.

Riesman has suggested that societal influence may be categorized according to three basic directions (1961). The first he calls the *"tradition-directed"* influence. This is a socialization process which is strongly influenced by the societal norms. The person who is tradition-directed attempts to conform to those norms and to understand them, and his behavior is structured according to the traditions of the culture. The second influence is that of *"inner-direction."* The person who follows this direction in the socialization process finds his behavior governed by attitudes which have been implanted by the societal elders and are usually directed toward certain general goals. The inner-directed person seeks to please authority in his socialization process and may accept a disciplinary approach to behavior. The third influence is that of *"other-direction."* The other-directed person will be socialized primarily by the direction he gets from his contemporaries and will tend to structure his behavior in accord with the expectations that others have for him.

results of socialization

As man is socialized, he discovers the self through interaction with his environment, in the course of which social judgments are made and evaluated. Socialization results in the creation of a self-image as a person judges himself in relation to what he believes others think about him. In addition, the socialization process also provides the matrix for the creation of what might be called the ideal-self. The individual tends to integrate his interpretation of societal expectations, the perfected experiences of others, and his wishes for such perfection, thereby identifying what he considers his ideal-self to be. When an individual's ideal-self is far removed from reality, and when such an image is accepted by the individual as being desirable and attainable, obvious problems will result.

Socialization also results in the creation of an ego, the recognition of the self as contrasted with the world outside the self. The ego is always a conscious part of the personality derived from the individual potential through contacts with reality in the socialization process. It is that facet of self which fosters confidence, recognition, and identification. Those societies which attempt to deprive the individual of ego also seek to foster the group's interests and to subjugate the individual to group effort and group goals. In any successful team action, there should be ego-involvement.

Because most of the interactions which significantly develop self are emotional in nature, experiences in the socialization process that have high emotional context are probably more meaningful than those that employ reason alone. It pays to "care" about things and to lose oneself in a cause, since the only way to really win life and self may be to lose them in the socialization process.

PERSONALITY

The identification of self through the socialization process creates the human personality. Allport noted that "personality is the dynamic organization within the individual of those psychophysical systems that determine his unique adjustments to his environment" (1937, p. 48). Newcomb believed that personality might be viewed as "the individual's organization of free dispositions to behavior" (1950, p. 277). We know that personality is the sum of a person's values and attitudes plus all of his traits, and that this sum is always a dynamic organization. The personality of the individual is governed by his continuous association with society and the cultural milieu. In a sense, personality is the subjective aspect of any society's culture.

Historically, personality has been viewed with respect to many indices. Probably the oldest index was that of the ancient humors. It was believed that these internal juices governed the disposition of man, and thus a person was dominated by whichever humor was most abundant within his being. The four humors were blood, phlegm, bile, and black bile, and even today we talk of a phlegmatic temperament, indicating a stolid and slow personality, or a bilious personality, suggesting a peevish nature.

There have been other attempts to relate personality to some physical or biological attribute, the most recent probably being that of William Sheldon, who sought to relate personality and temperament to morphological char-

acteristics and suggested distinct personality characteristics for the ecto-
morph, the mesomorph, and the endomorph (1942).

All of the attempts to find a purely hereditary base for personality have
fallen far short of their purposed paradigm. The establishment of personality appears not to be so simple as a theory of genetic transfer might indicate.

It has also been proposed that personality is a product of environmental
circumstance, a view which was supported by the great educational theorist,
John Dewey. More recently, the majority of explanations of personality
formation contend that personality is a result of the cultural forces acting on
the individual, although it is apparent that heredity can limit the effect of
the culture, just as there are times when the cultural environment places
limits on a hereditary disposition. There is always a difference between the
personality potential and the realized personality, and this difference is usually created by the interplay of heredity and environment.

influences and determinants

There are two basic current concepts with regard to personality determination. The first is that proposed by Sigmund Freud and his followers—namely,
that the individual is motivated by the pleasure principle, which is concerned
with physiological satisfactions (1930). This principle is in constant conflict
with the collective social conscience of society. Thus, the egoistic principle of
self is antagonistic to the altruistic principle of society. Therefore, according
to Freud, the ego battles the superego, or the individual battles society. From
this warfare, personality evolves.

The second theory was suggested by Charles Cooley and his associates
(1902). According to Cooley, personality develops as a product of socialization, especially through interactions which involve "face-to-face" contact.
Cooley believed that the individual always reacts in terms of his perception
of what others believe him to be. Thus, the self and personality are always
social, and Cooley used the term "looking-glass self" to describe and make
lucid this concept. It was surmised that the self exists only in relation to
others.

Obviously, both of these theories have some validity. Personality constantly
seeks both inner and outer stability. This stability requires a previous history of life experience, and these experiences are both personalized and
socialized.

In the structuring of the personality there are certain biological factors
which cannot be ignored. The body structure of the individual is of great
importance. Recent work in the concept of body image attests to the fact
that personality is partially developed in relation to the way a person thinks
that he looks in his biological shell. A man's reflexes are also vital in personality development as are physiological drives to fulfill needs, prevailing
moods as influenced by the endocrine system, and the innate capacities which
govern learning potential. Biological maturation must occur before the fully
developed personality is produced. This is not to infer that children are
lacking in personality structure, but rather that the child has not arrived at
any form of stable personality, and that such stability cannot be expected at
least until after maturity has been reached, if then.

There is no way to predict what effects heredity, biological disposition, or environment will have in terms of personality for any individual. Intelligence, social aptitude, motivation, timing, and the socialized culture norms all influence behavior and thus are adjuncts to the development of personality.

The acquisition of a personality is governed by the drives of the individual, the cues which he acknowledges, the human response and the rewards or punishments which are offered. These are primary biological aspects of personality. In addition, there are the secondary or acquired drives which are social in nature and which are rivals of, and may even supplant, the primary motives as the basis for learning how to act.

Kluckhohn and Murray have suggested that personality is the result of four classes of personality determinants (1954). The first is a *constitutional* determinant, which is governed by the biological and physiological components of human nature. The second is the determinant of *group membership*, which structures the role that the individuals must play in situations. The third determinant is *role* itself, which is both public and private in nature and governed by such things as sex, age, occupation, and skill. The fourth determinant is a *situational* one, whereby the personality comes into being as events occur and leave their mark.

The stable or balanced personality maintains a relatively positive self-conception; his rules and norms do not conflict with other rules and norms, so that role may be fairly constant. For stability and balance, it is also quite important that the gap between aspiration and achievement be relatively narrow and that society and culture allow some means for "gap reduction."

It should be noted that the American culture encourages personality conflict. This is not because of the complex organization of the cultural pattern, as one might suspect, but because individual values oppose moral norms and because social structure opposes social values (1956). Personality deviation is one of the prices that Americans must pay for a cultural system that encourages personal freedom. It seems a small price to pay for liberty and independence.

values

Society benefits from personality development as does the individual. The abstract sentiments which reflect personality also tend to support societal standards and reinforce values. Hence, the traditional love of God, flag, and country may be manifested in the patriotic fever of an individual personality, and such patriotism in turn supports the societal structure and reinforces the cultural directive found in the Judeo-Christian ethic. Moral norms are also a result of personality development, just as they are tools of socialization which help formulate personality. Self-conception, the focal motivational point of personality, lends to American society the individualism which is its basic pattern.

Almost all important social institutions are reflections of personality forces. Games and athletic events may well be a residue of a less differentiated societal pattern, or they may be the creation of composite personality structures which need such an outlet and institution to serve their development. Personality may also be a factor in the integration of social institutions. Thus, the personal desire for excitement and novelty might foster integration links between home and community, community and nation, nation and home. It is Kaplan's view that personality usually supports the social system and lends it strength (1957, Chap. 4).

types of personality

The personality structure of an individual must integrate psychological, biological, and sociological behavior patterns and reactions. The *biogenic personality* facet is characterized by the anatomy and physiology of the individual, his instincts, reflexes, and intelligence, as expressed through emotional adjustments and ideology. The *psychogenic personality* facet arises out of those experiences not involving other people as social beings, and the *sociogenic personality* facet is best characterized through role playing in society and the recognition of a conscious private world. Of these three facets of personality, the sociogenic role is the most easily modified and thus supports change and innovation to a greater degree than all other facets.

Any culture tends to support the concept of what might be called a "model personality" or a "representative personality." This is a syndrome of qualities which reflects and has been created by the cultural standards. Thus, we have what might be an identifiable "all-American" type of person; we talk of the "German type," the "French type," the "British type," the "scholar type," and the "athlete type." Each of these generalizations brings to mind a picture of a model personality which may or may not actually exist.

personality behavior

Personality can only be observed through behavior. Berne has suggested that the individual has what he calls a "stimulus hunger," a desire to be touched and stroked (1964). This turns to a "recognition hunger" which makes demands for attention and identification. Both stimulus and recognition foster a "structure hunger," a need to organize and structure one's waking hours. Berne believes that these hungers precipitate three distinguishable types of programmed behavior. The first he calls internally programmed, or *archaeopsychic,* behavior. Such behavior involves dreams, fantasies, delusional thinking, and flight from reality. The second type of behavior is probability programmed, or *neopsychic,* behavior. Such behavior is manifested in the normal activities and procedures involved in living. The third type of behavior is what is called socially programmed, or *partly extrapsychic,* behavior. Such behavior finds its outlets in rituals, pastimes, operational maneuvers, and games. Each of the programmed behaviors serves the hungers in some way.

Thus, it is apparent that personality is both a reflection and an instigator of behavior. It most often involves a process of interaction between people, for social contact relieves tensions and helps maintain personality equilibrium.

ROLE PLAYING

Shakespeare once said that "all the world's a stage, and all the men and women merely players. They have their exits and their entrances; and one man in his time plays many parts." So it is that role playing is the mediator between societal requirements and individual behavior as manifested through personality. The player, man, usually seeks a role that is congenial to himself, knowing full well that the role will bring influences to bear upon himself. In the American society there is usually some freedom of choice with regard to roles, and although certain roles are inflicted upon us, there are equally as many that we have a chance to accept or reject.

influences

The roles that are chosen usually are those from which satisfactions are expected. The appropriate role behavior for any specific situation is elicited through the operation of a system which offers both positive and negative sanctions, or rewards and punishments. Positive role sanction (reward) is often in terms of money, fame, status, and other attributes of success. Negative sanction (punishment) is most often found in some sort of shame or ill fortune. Acceptance of a role is accompanied by identification with the moral order of the society, a respect for legitimate authority, and a strong feeling of obligation to live up to the expectation of the society. Each of these guides to role behavior may also be the motivation for role behavior.

A young woman in a college situation may play the role of student, choosing this role because she believes that it gives her status and will help her achieve financial independence at some future date. Her behavior, as a college student, is influenced by society's expectations for the college student and by her respect for the rules and regulations of an academic world which has the power to grant degrees as a symbol of success.

Likewise, the young boy who chooses to play the role of athlete on the high school team often chooses his role because it is a way to status and fame. The role of athlete is formulated by the expectations that society has for the athlete in terms of physical prowess and personality attributes. In addition, there are rules and regulations which govern team membership and the right of a player to call himself an athlete. These rules must be acknowledged and adhered to if the role is to be acceptable to the society.

conflict

Because "one man in his time plays many parts," there is bound to be conflict within and between roles. The roles themselves present problems. First, there is the problem of role recruitment. All roles are not automatically filled, and it is up to society to make the role attractive enough to encourage people to seek it. Currently, there is difficulty in recruiting people for the role of teacher, especially that of woman physical education teacher. In such cases the role needs to be made more attractive so that societal values can be identified with the role, thereby tempting people to assume it.

The second problem that roles present is that of succession. There have to be understudies ready and willing to take over the role when the main actors abandon the part, and often it is necessary to have rules set up which will govern succession. There has to be a plan whereby new athletes are found for a team. The educational institutions which support athletic teams usually have one way of providing for succession and the professional teams have another. If there are no understudies or rules for succession, the societal role will tend to disappear.

Yet another problem regarding role playing involves its traditional aspect. As a role changes from era to era, it is very difficult to keep players who know what they are doing and to determine how the role identification can be portrayed accurately to others who might aspire to assume the role. For example, the role of chaperone has undergone radical changes and is still in a state of transition. The role of chaperone has moved from that of a policing agent to that of an understanding friend to that of an acknowledged nuisance. This is a rapid and disquieting transition which has happened so fast that the role is now difficult to define; so it is equally as difficult to find people who are willing to assume such a nebulous and undesirable role.

Yet another problem of role playing is in connection with the *rites de passage,* the ceremonies performed when an individual passes from one role to another. The marriage ceremony is one of the oldest forms of *rites de passage.* There is also the graduation ceremony, the puberty ceremonies of certain religions, and the numerous recognition and "moving up" occasions which are fostered by society. Of late, less attention has been paid to some of these ceremonies than formerly, so it is becoming increasingly difficult for an individual to know when he has moved from one role to another. One of the very real problems in the United States is the general lack of *rites de passage* regarding social maturity. The magic age of eighteen is usually thought of as the dividing point from adolescence to maturity, and the age of twenty-one is regarded as full-fledged adulthood because it carries with it a certain legal status. However, lately there has been the belief that adulthood may start at the age of sixteen since that is the age at which a driver's license may be obtained in most states. There is confusion regarding adulthood privileges because there is no clearly defined identification of role change.

Conflict in roles is often caused by an attitude, a tendency to act in some special way in any given situation. Overt behavior does not always reveal attitude. Very often attitudes are ambivalent, so that a person may have more than one attitude about the same thing. Such ambivalence makes role playing that much more difficult and often results in personality conflict or cultural conflict between the individual and society.

A certain amount of role conflict is supported by society and adds to the spice of living. It is difficult to know when to play the role of counselor and teacher and when to play the role of friend and confidant. The line between these two conflicting roles is crooked and faint, and it takes all of the wits of the individuals involved to ascertain where the limits of each role are to be found. It should be pointed out that not all dual roles are conflictual. It is possible to have complementary roles which foster reciprocal attitudes and behavior patterns. Certainly the complementary roles of husband-father or wife-mother have more reciprocal parts than they have conflicting parts. So the roles of athlete and student or of teacher and friend can have complementary aspects which can be capitalized upon as readily as the conflictual aspects can be emphasized.

INTERACTION

Role players must ultimately interact with other role players, and such interaction always involves norms, status positions, and reciprocal obligations. Interaction can result in cooperation, competition, or conflict. The actualization of interaction produces interdependence and balance among all aspects of nature and of man's roles.

Communication between players may be either direct or indirect and is usually accomplished through the means of symbols and symbolic behavior. Role behavior, attitude, and idealization of concepts all have their origins in primary interaction. All interacting individuals influence each other, and the person who has played a passive role is as much an influence as the one who plays an active role.

In dealing with the socialization process and the consequent development of personality, or with the interaction fostered by role playing, we must not forget the capacity of the individual for independent action. Man is not socialized as easily as laboratory white mice, for each man retains within himself some divine spark which indeed allows him still to be "master of my fate" and "captain of my soul."

IMPLICATIONS FOR PHYSICAL EDUCATION

All facets of a society are concerned with man's cultural potential, and physical education is no exception. The socialization process, with the resulting personality development, seems to have a special fascination for physical education. This might be explained in terms of the symbolic behavior supported by physical education. Movement is a symbol of personality and self-concept, and since movement is physical education's special interest, it is logical that it concern itself with personality. In addition, the concept of organic integrity both affects the concept of self and allows for the mobility necessary for the role playing in the socialization process. Finally, physical education's stake in man's cultural potential affects the concept of play. Games are among the most socialized attributes of any society and are an integral part of the cultural heritage. Games utilize the concept of role playing and thus can be thought of as basic socialization methods and personality formulators.

Ireland suggests that it might be possible to use the recreational or play maturation hierarchy to help diagnose medical and psychiatric disorders (1959, pp. 356–60). He observed that the infant is interested in solitary and egocentric play; the preschooler is interested in small group and sporadic socialization play; the adolescent is interested in both small and large groups; his play involves both sexes and assumes certain play prejudices; the young adult has the same play standards as the adolescent, but adds to his play in the use of the sedentary small group; the middle-aged adult continues with the play interests of the young adult and finds in these interests certain cultural orientations; and finally, the older adult regresses to certain early recreation patterns but with greater cognition as to their meaning. Ireland suggests that if a person is not playing within his proper level, it might indicate behavioral difficulty.

Shugart reports that people who were admitted to a neuropsychiatric ward in a naval hospital had had meager play experiences (1955, pp. 204–9). Symonds suggests that the greatest need for normal adolescent boys and girls is the opportunity for social participation and the greatest personality handicap is social isolation (1948, pp. 163–69). Obviously the game concept makes provision for social participation and minimizes social isolation.

Thrasher says that phyiscal prowess is important in determining leadership, but he believes that it is not vital, for it was possible for his gang leaders to achieve their role with daring decisiveness and brains (1936). In relation to this, Biddulph reported that students with high athletic achievement had a greater degree of personal adjustment (1954, pp. 1–7). This observation was supported by Reaney, who reported that 600 boys and girls who were better than average in playing games were also superior in intelligence and general social ability (1914, pp. 226–252). Rarick and McKee lent further support to the relationship between personality and motor efficiency when they reported that third grade children who had high motor proficiency were better adjusted in school and possessed a greater amount of ease with regard to personal relationships (1949, pp. 148–52). Cowell and Ismail contend that boys and girls with high physical measures had strong leadership potentials (1962, pp. 40–43).

Peoples' attitudes and ideals have their origins in primary interaction, and games allow such an opportunity. It has long been noted that a game may be a simplified reproduction of life itself, permitting a person to test himself against unknown odds to see if he is wanting. Games are primary forms of the socialization process and thus may foster conflict. In specific situations, the player may sacrifice all for the team or the team may stultify the individual's potential for group action.

Athletics create a status position which influences personality and ameliorates socialization. Games also demand discipline. They have rules and boundaries and they exact from an individual his best effort, his finest role.

Movement is the overt interpretation of personality and relates the self to others through a symbol language that has meaning.

In structuring a game situation, a child sets the stage for man's cultural potential. What part each participant wants to play depends upon the socialization process, upon personality development, and upon the interaction of role-playing people. One may want to be the first baseman for the afternoon, and in playing that role one adds a dimension to the self which would not have been possible without that experience. The part one chooses to play is an individual expression of selfhood. It incorporates all of the wishes, desires, potentialities, and understandings of man, and we are fortunate indeed that we have the concept of games to place the life experience in a simpler, more easily understood form.

IV

Man's
Social Groups

"Which team you gonna take?"

It has been suggested, at times, that man is a gregarious animal, tending to herd and flock like cattle or chickens. There is some degree of truth in that suggestion, but it appears that man's motives for gregariousness differ from those of other animals.

Humans seek groups in which to live because they have found that group living not only helps them best to sustain and maintain themselves but it also permits and encourages efficiency of operation and personal excellence with regard to tasks. The concept of labor division is an important one in man's decision to form himself into groups. There is not time for an individual to do all of the things necessary for racial survival, so humans come together to facilitate the labor and to insure perfected results.

The social groups of man are imperative to the social order. They maintain the institutions of marriage and family, religion, government, education, and social conscience. Specific social relationships emerged because of the cardinal needs of a society. Such relationships, resulting in social groups, have answered those needs successfully. It appears that there are common social groups which are identified with special social institutions which are a permanent fixture of all societies of men.

A group can be defined as two or more persons who interact with one another over a more or less appreciable and continual period; who are mutually aware of each other as members of the group; who are able to communicate effectively with each other by some acceptable means; and who have established a definite "interpersonal structure" which enables them to share a common purpose.

The essence of the group is interaction, and toward this end the group seeks to establish channels of communication. The composite group works out the roles that the group demands, it agrees upon functions, it sets certain goals, it regulates behavior, and it exists unto itself as a whole and complete entity. The formation of a group is a deliberate social action; not an instinctive behavior. Herein man differs markedly from cattle and chickens.

The universal bases upon which groups are structured are sex, age, kinship, common residence, and voluntary association. These universals are found in all societies, and it is to be expected that they will exist whether they are overtly acknowledged or not. Hence, it is foolish to assume, for example, that there will be no sex role-oriented groups in a cultural pattern. Certain age levels tend to identify with one another, especially during the maturing years, and common background fostered by common residence will surely facilitate group formation. It is an unwise teacher who attempts to ignore the universal grouping of people. Coeducation, rejection of age grouping, and regional and ethnic integration all have their place, but they are in opposition to fundamental patterns of group organization and are difficult to support and maintain.

Groups differ from *categories* in that categories refer to a number of people who are thought of together but who are not necessarily a group. Baseball players as opposed to basketball players represent categories, while a group would be the American League baseball players or a specific university's basketball team.

Groups also differ from *aggregations* in that an aggregation is a number of people who are held together by bonds other than communication. A busload of people or a theater audience may be an aggregation. Aggregations seldom care about one another unless an emergency occurs, and then the close proximity of the individuals might cause them to become a group.

Ordinarily, voluntary groups are formed with regard to personal attraction of members for each other, the prestige that the group can command, and the sort of task that needs to be performed.

GROUP CHARACTERISTICS

Groups always must have some sort of boundary maintenance. The boundaries suggest a sort of "specialness" for the group and often help to give a group status. Personal needs must be met by the group, or it will have no reason for being. A group has to offer a considerable amount of influence, for if it is possible for an individual to have the same influence without group support, there will be no need for the group formation. The group also provides for an identification of "consciousness of kind." This is a process in which group members recognize each other and find in that recognition certain satisfactions which come from their unity. There are times when a group can create its own legends, myths, and models, and this enhances group solidarity and serves to characterize the group. Good groups have high morale which is fostered by exemplary leadership, faith in the leader and in each other, organizational efficiency, and faith and confidence that all members of the group will share in the distribution of the "reward" which is the group goal.

Group stability depends upon the fact that there will be only a gradual turnover in the group personnel, that the group owns physical property, that traditions and ideals are connected with the group, that there is a code of behavior which is expected and enforced by the group, and that there is organized leadership.

There often is a tendency for a group to feel so secure in its characteristics that it maintains itself after the need has disappeared. Thus, we have the "old gang" who used to play ball together continuing to meet long after their ballplaying days are over. People tend to hold onto groups that had meaning to them, so that at times it is harder to dissolve an old group than to form a new one.

It is not absolutely necessary for a group to have physical proximity, although this usually facilitates the interaction. However, if proximity is not possible, then there must be the opportunity for psychological interaction which supports either agreement or disagreement. Some of the professional organizations such as the American Medical Association, the American Association for Health, Physical Education, and Recreation, and the National Association for Physical Education of College Women all are examples of groups which encourage only limited proximity, but which endorse psychological interaction through both agreement and disagreement.

TYPES OF GROUPS

There is almost always an identity pattern for any group. This pattern is really part of a larger continuum of identification which helps to type and codify a group and yet does not limit its dynamic disposition. Mercer has suggested that groups may be categorized as small or extended, primary or secondary, permanent or transient, formal or informal, and horizontal or vertical (1958). An example of a small group would be the bowling team representing a community center, while the extended group is exemplified by the American Bowling Congress. A primary group is one that enjoys face-to-face contacts, and an example of this might be the neighborhood gang, as opposed to the secondary group of the municipal Parks and Recreation Bureau. A permanent group might be the Boy or Girl Scouts of America, while a transient group would be the annual scout jamboree. Formal groups might be represented by the United States Field Hockey Association, while an example of an informal group is the Saturday afternoon hockey for interested housewives. Vertical groups are exemplified by the Officiating Services Area of the Division for Girls and Women's Sports, where leadership and status are attained by vertical mobility within the group structure. Thus, you advance from an intramural official to a local official, to a national official. Horizontal groups might be the Division of Men's Athletics or the Division for Girls and Women's Sports of the American Association for Health, Physical Education, and Recreation. In each of these Divisions, leadership, status, and membership are given a horizontal spread. Each division is "equal" to the other and each job within the division carries "equal status." There is no sure way of "moving up".

Groups may be deliberately structured to be *purposive* in that they have a set goal which must be accomplished within a given amount of time. The goal can be quite specific, such as earning enough money to buy lights for the athletic field; or it can have a more expansive and nebulous definition, such as insuring play opportunities for all school children during out-of-school time.

Ordinarily, a group tends to *expand the interests* of any individual within it. Although the task may have attracted the person to the group, the interests of the group are greater than the task, and the individual, upon joining, must expand his own interests and understandings in order to remain a part of the group.

There are some groups which are highly *selective* about their membership and usually only allow those persons to join whom the group thinks are qualified. Athletic teams are an example of such groups, as are such social groups as fraternities, sororities, and the local country club. In a group where selectivity is paramount with regard to the membership, there are rigid and set rules which govern the selective process, and there is usually a committee within the group which controls the organization of the selection.

Groups may be *involuntary* as far as membership is concerned. An individual joins a family group by virtue of his kinship, which is involuntary. Nationality groups are usually involuntary, as are groups which are based upon regional affiliation and residence.

In America, especially, many groups are *voluntary*. These groups are joined because the individual believes that he has much to gain from, and much to give to, the purposes of the group. Thus, we have the voluntary affiliations of many people with the Red Cross, the Community Chest, the American Kennel Club, and the Young Men's or Young Women's Christian Association.

GROUP ORGANIZATION

A group may be as simple as a twosome, which is known as a *dyad*. In such a group, organization is kept at a minimum. However, when groups assume the proportions of *triads* or larger multiples, some type of organization is essential and implicit in the group's characteristics and purposes. Once there are three people involved in a group, the third person is the mediator for any disagreement, represents the balance of power, and may initiate conflicts. It is important to note that the "third person" may be a different person for each situation within a triad, but there is always the "three's-a-crowd" situation with which to deal.

As the society grows more complex, one finds more organizations and more groups formed to take care of the complexity. It would appear that organizations always call forth more organizations. If there is a group formed to represent the interests of society on one side of a controversy, so there must be another group formed to present the other side. As groups become more highly organized and differentiated, so they tend to splinter and seek ways in which smaller interests can be served. The proliferation of a large group spawns a multitude of smaller groups, each with the potential of later proliferation. An excellent example of this is the growth of the American Association for Health, Physical Education, and Recreation. As the membership and interests of the group have expanded, the organization has become more complex until now there is such diversity of concern and such complicated organization that group identification is increasingly difficult and serious thought has been given to division within the organization so that specific interests may be served to best advantage.

There is also a tendency for voluntary groups to become formal groups. Thus, the sandlot baseball team, with parental guidance, associates with the Municipal Recreation Department, and the Municipal Recreation Department affiliates with the Little League organization, and soon the sandlot team has a status and organization which dictates rules of membership, ways to play, and incentives and rewards which had not really been sought by the individual within the group, but had been initiated by the total group.

Unquestionably, certain affiliations made by individuals during their college years result in affiliation with groups that the individuals never dreamed that they supported. This can be especially frightening and puzzling when the group, in later years, assumes an aura that it did not have at the time that the individual chose to join it. The "Communist front" groups are examples of such a problem.

As the group organization gains complexity, it is possible for the group to turn away from its original aims and goals and assume new ones. This is usually a gradual process and has a tendency to be evolutionary rather than revolutionary. The athletic "Letter Club" may become the high school "Leaders Club" or the "Home and Garden Club" may become the "Jaycettes" of the community.

The day by day decisions of an organization are often interpreted as the commitments and precedents of that organization. Usually there is little attention paid the day by day procedures until such time as the group realizes that precedent has been set.

Groups can be either centralized or decentralized in organization. The larger the organization, the more ranks there are within the organization, but not necessarily the greater the centralization. According to Berelson and Steiner, the greater the decentralization, the more discordance there is within the group but the greater tolerance there is for the discord (1964). The greater the decentralization, the better identity the group has with its rank-and-file members. A crisis within a group almost always promotes centralization of that group and usually initiates causes for group communication which might not have existed before. For example, a class which is decentralized in nature, once the teacher is removed, might seek centralization if it found itself accused of bizarre behavior or social impropriety. In such a case, the class might organize itself, seek to centralize, and find reason for communication within the class that had not existed before.

Communication proceeds both up and down a group hierarchy. It is essential that communication be handed down the hierarchy if the group purposes are to be fulfilled, but communication up the hierarchy, though desirable, is not essential. The more formal the organization and structure of the group, the less upward flow of communication. It is usual for the people on the top to insist upon productivity from the group, while the people on the bottom of the hierarchy usually seek more personal consideration. Thus, the coach of the team expects his boys "to play their hearts out" to win the game for dear old *alma mater*. The team will assume some of the desires of the coach, but also desires to enjoy the game situation, to be granted privileges for team membership, and to reap the reward of a successful season in terms of status and prestige.

The closer the membership requirements are to the individual's interests, the longer the individual will remain a part of a group. Thus, many boys and girls "grow out" of the scouting movement. In response to such a situation, the scouting groups have endeavored to serve more mature interests with programs which stress community service and world understanding.

Sometimes it is foolish to attempt to hold a group together when the interests of the individuals are no longer served. This is certainly the problem of many Alumni Associations. The primary interest of the individual is not with his institution of learning after his formal education is over. Therefore, Alumni Associations attempt to stress "duty" and "obligation" to the past as their rationale for membership and, failing in this, they seek to serve the individual's new interests by giving him certain types of status and privilege associated with the university or college. The former student may purchase tickets to the athletic contests and get preferential treatment as to location of seats and availability of tickets. Often a Department of Athletics and Physical Education is forced to become the associate of the Alumni Association group, usually with the promise that the rewards will be shared by both groups.

Small, informal, hostile groups can oppose the organization of a large group and may either destroy it or cause drastic change within its organization. It should be possible for people to "resign" from a group. If such a principle is possible, opposition within the group is usually constructive and friendly rather than hostile. If resignation is impossible, such as from family groups, it stands to reason that individual neurotic behavior will probably result. Such behavior is the only individual defense mechanism that a person has, and it is his protest to the world regarding his enforced membership.

It would be foolish to believe that all groups, even all voluntary groups, are essentially congenial. Congeniality does not always foster worth in a group. It does seem reasonable, however, to believe that all groups should foster personal respect between members. This respect can tolerate controversy, foster understanding, and facilitate interaction.

GROUP STRUCTURE

Groups not only have characteristics, organization, and types, but they also have structure. The structure is usually based upon a social setting which gives meaning to the group. Merrill believed that there were five basic social settings which fostered certain types of group structure (1965).

gemeinschaft vs. gesellschaft

The *Gemeinschaft* setting was thought of, in the past, essentially as a rural setting characterized by kinship, familiarity, and friendship relationships; while the *Gesellschaft* setting was that of an urban culture characterized by a rational concern for the individual, but with relatively impersonal relationships.

It is hard to categorize urban and rural cultures today. Technological advances have broken down many of the basic characteristics of such living groups. The automobile, the mass communication instruments, the cooperative apartment ventures, and many other artifacts of technology have confused what was once a clear and lucid picture of the "country mouse" and the "city mouse." However, the concept of the social setting is still valid and can help with certain identifications of group structure.

secular vs. sacred

There are certain secular societies which welcome change and continually attempt to incorporate such change in their group structure. There are other societies, more sacred in origin, which are resistant to change and attempt to outlaw it. Many "ritual groups," convinced that there is but one way to act, accept the principle that "what was good enough for my ancestors is good enough for me." Certain of the "cause" groups, such as the Temperance League, proceed under such sacred auspices. There are also times when professional organizations tend to be sacred in terms of their social setting. This can occur easily when the membership is selective. On the other hand, secular groups may change with such facility that the basic security of group endeavor may be broken down. A professional organization which beats every new drum and hops aboard every fascinating bandwagon will not add any stability to its responsibility for established tasks.

homogeneity vs. heterogeneity

The social setting for a group may be one that calls together all like elements within society and unites around such a homogeneous concept; or it may be a setting which encourages people of unlike nature to come together and find a common task or cause in their heterogeneous characteristics.

complete vs. segmental

A setting which supports a complete group is one that is interested in primary relationships. In such a complete setting, all is known about individuals within the group structure. Families, communities, and basic play groups are characterized by completeness. A segmental group is fostered by a setting that is concerned only with the specific aspects of individual behavior which will affect the welfare of the group or of the total society. For example, a group with a special interest in certain recreational opportunities such as swimming, in organizing the Swim Club, is seldom interested in the political or educational affiliations of its members; it is interested only in that segment of the individual which affects the Swim Club, namely the individual's interest in swimming.

anonymity vs. familiarity

In a social setting which undergirds anonymity, there is a tendency for the individual to be lost in the crowd and to be included in the group only because of certain material aspects. A setting which fosters familiarity will judge the completeness of the individual on the familiar terms of family, work, and home. We often join groups, such as charitable organizations, in which we purposively seek anonymity. We are content to make a financial donation to the group but wish no additional involvement. There are other times when familiarity is sought, so that as we become a part of a neighborhood drive or endeavor, we want to know the people with whom we are associating and what they represent.

GROUP CLASSIFICATION

Groups have been classified under many headings, and each scheme seeks to develop a descriptive analysis of a group. Basically, the classification has been with reference to "we" and "us" groups—that is, groups which utilize the rationale of primary involvement as opposed to secondary involvement.

primary groups

The primary group is based on a universal human relationship which could not be avoided even if one wished to avoid it. Faris states that the primary group "is a changing organization of functional activities tending toward an end, influenced by its past, and guided by its purposes and its future" (1932, p. 50). The family, the play group, the adolescent clique, the gang, and adult friendship groups are all examples of primary groups.

NATURE. The primary group is mainly concerned with face-to-face relationships, and all interaction occurs with respect to such an intimate relationship. The interaction is usually marked by spontaneity, and the group represents a place where man can "be himself" with a minimum of role playing. The primary group is the place where a person is most drastically socialized and made to understand the cultural heritage of the society. The real nature of the group lies in its organization. It does not depend upon spatial contiguity, but instead upon a type of functional interaction. The primary group needs memories to give meaning to its existence and it needs purposes to guarantee its future. Cooley, who first described the primary group and its nature, says that the primary group is an "intimate face-to-face association and cooperation ... the product of long and intimate interaction under informal conditions ... a group that is not joined ... a certain fusion of individualities in a common whole so that one's very self ... is the common life and purpose of the group" (1909, pp. 23–27).

To all those who are members of a primary group, the group association itself is of as much value as the activities that the group undertakes. The thing that primary group members care about most is that they are members and that they do things together as a group. There are times when there is real primary group hunger on the part of an individual; where he cares more about being included in the group than he cares about the task of the group. When being "in" counts more than anything else, this hunger can result in individuals participating in activities that they really do not desire or even endorse.

FORMS. Primary groups assume many different forms. Besides the family group, there is probably no primary relationship that is more important to an individual than that of his association with a *peer group*. It is a volunteer group, usually structured according to age and interest characteristics, and providing an intimate and powerful social setting for personality development. The peer group has many identities in terms of age and purpose, but it usually has its own board of admission and it is characterized by "togetherness." The peer group trains the individual to get along within the societal structure. It is not as indulgent as the family, nor as understanding. As it teaches the individual the social attributes, it is strict in its admonitions and not permissive about behavioral patterns. The peer group tends to develop a rational conscience for its members and it assists in creating the opportunities for emotional independence. A peer group will not tolerate "running home to mother." You have to be able to "take it" yourself and face the basic loneliness of emotional selfhood.

The *reference group* is a primary group to which the individual refers but does not belong. He is "out" rather than "in" although he longs to be "in." The reference group is often utilized by marginal persons—those who are attempting to gain entree into a primary group because they have left another such group. Such a tenuous position is difficult and can foster behavioral problems. The child who wants "in" with respect to a certain neighborhood play group will attempt almost any type of behavior to be recognized and to be invited to participate.

Primary groups usually have a hierarchy established in terms of leadership and prestige. These hierarchies are often related to age, sex, physical prowess, morphology, and personality attributes.

BASIC FUNCTIONS. The primary group is organized to assist in creating possibilities for human activity. Man must have a reason for existence, and primary groups support reasons for life. They also provide the means by which such activities can take place. The primary group is interested in the defense of the individual. The group tends to protect the individual from both physical and psychological harm and gives him security. The primary group also is the facet of society which maintains a friendly and congenial, but strict, atmosphere for personality development. Finally, the primary group is the citadel of communication, keeping its individual members alert to the communications of the total society.

LIABILITIES. Primary group associations have certain liabilities which come to bear upon the individual. The first is the restrictive aspects of the primary group. The group likes to keep its members to itself and restricts their mobility in society. An individual is expected to "come home" when he is in trouble or when he encounters any sort of emotional upset. The primary group guards and possesses its membership with fervor and zeal, and it does not readily release its members to other groups, even if such release means the formation of another primary group. The desire of parents to hold onto their children, the identification of what has been called "Momism," and Daddy's unwillingness to let daughter choose a marriage partner are all examples of the possessiveness of the family group and the restrictions that such a group can place on an individual. Not quite as severe or drastic is the sort of restriction that organized play groups put upon their membership. If you belong to a certain team you are not allowed to play with, or even associate with, people from other teams, and all team problems are to be taken to the coach rather than any outside agent.

Another liability of primary group association is the insistence upon conformity. Primary groups like and endorse group standards that approach what they interpret as being "normal." There is little ambivalence within a primary group, for the roles are so clearly defined that the individual takes on the personality description of the role. The coach likes his boys to all look alike, act alike, and be alike as far as their team image is concerned. The gang will oust any person who is not willing to conform to its standards of dress and behavior, the family expects a certain conformity of behavior with regard to the role of family membership.

Another liability of the primary group is that it tends to be sacred, familiar, complete, and homogeneous. It resists change and reacts against innovation. These characteristics are being changed in modern society—so much so, as a matter of fact, that many social scientists fear that the primary group is beginning to vanish from the societal picture. Of great concern is the question as to what social structure will assume the basic functions of the primary group.

OUTCOMES. The outcomes that accrue from primary group membership, obviously, reflect the functions of the group. However, the group itself, regardless of its particular function, has value within any society. It supports the concept that there is a place where uniqueness can count, for in spite of its fascination with conformity, the primary group permits a certain degree of uniqueness and thus encourages the individual to become experimental and innovative. The individual gains the opportunity to formulate a self-image, and the primary group, more than any other facet of society, helps with the personality identification of its members. The group itself has an identity in the total pattern of society, for society is partially structured on the identification of its primary groups. The primary group also protects the individual member by reinterpreting and modifying goals and rules and by adapting them to the individual. The primary group fosters adjustment on the part of the society as well as on the part of the individual. There are numerous times when this type of grouping encourages an altruistic attitude toward society and, with the establishment of such attitudes, society itself is enriched.

secondary groups

The secondary group is a contrived societal scheme. It basks in the cultural milieu and is created and subsidized by society. It is essential in the cultural picture, for it gives a past and present to the total society and also sets up indications for the future. Secondary groups revolve around politics, religion, economics, social causes, and all of the other aspects of living with which a society concerns itself.

NATURE. The secondary group is more inclusive than the primary group and hence tends to be less intimate and personal. It does not need face-to-face contact in order to exist. Secondary group participation usually infers that all relationships are entered into voluntarily on the part of the members and that such membership implies that there was a purpose for joining the secondary group. The purposes usually are related to the fact that the membership feels that there should be a distribution of power, there should be the experience of participation, and that such grouping is necessary in order to effect social change. In short, many people feel that there is little hope for a lone voice "crying in the wilderness," but that strength can be gained by uniting. So they join a secondary group.

The secondary group members regard each other as means to an end and know that in this type of grouping people can be replaced, for no one is so unique that he is indispensable. Secondary group membership usually rests upon the concept of a contract. The member believes that his personal liability to the group is only with reference to the contract. Therefore, it is necessary for the secondary group member to react to any given situation only with that part of his personal commitment which he had pledged by contract upon joining the group.

FORMS. The forms of secondary groups are many, involving all aspects of society which are not concerned with primary group membership. Thus, secondary groups tend to be secular, heterogeneous, segmental, and anonymous. They have clearly defined purposes which are very often task-oriented. They are usually the products of an affluent society, and findings have indicated that secondary groups do not emerge until primary groups have abandoned their functions, or have so completely fulfilled them that there is the time and energy for secondary grouping. Thus, we might reasonably expect to find in a country such as the United States a proliferation of secondary group memberships. Less differentiated and less complex cultures do not have the secondary groups available that are found in the American cultural pattern.

BASIC FUNCTIONS. The secondary group allows and encourages people to participate meaningfully in activities of a mass society. It structures and gives strength and depth to social interaction, and it provides organization for social change. It is the only organized outlet for causes bigger than the intimate identification pattern provided by the primary group. It frees the individual from certain personal responsibilities with regard to decision making and gives him freedom for invention, change, and innovation.

The secondary group provides challenge and competition for the individual with no quarter given. It functions to give the individual the room for development not always permitted in the primary group. The secondary group seldom stifles an individual; it gives him license to be what he wishes within the boundaries set by the group's membership.

LIABILITIES. The impersonal aspects of the secondary group make it much less essential than the primary group, so it is possible for people to live with little or no reference to secondary groups. It has been estimated that at least half of the population of the United States has very limited association with any secondary groups. The group seldom demands an accounting for individual behavior, and thus it is often unable to inflict any sort of control upon its members or to effect discipline. Positive and negative sanctions tend to be nebulous and can be easily ignored. Because the secondary group "cares less" about the individual, the individual cares less about the secondary group. Secondary groups are very often transient, and while they lend novelty to society and its cultural heritage, they do not add to the basic stability and security which a society often seeks.

Often a secondary group attempts to bring about a primary group relationship among its members, and when this happens confusion and difficulties can result. For example, if a Department of Health, Physical Education, and Recreation in a university system attempts to set up a primary relationship between its faculty and students, the students may rebel because they did not count on a secondary group assuming primary group responsibilities. On the other hand, the students might welcome such a relationship and feel that the faculty was especially interested in them as people. But if this is done, then the department must be more understanding than any secondary group normally should be about the personal security and problems of its majors, and must seek ways to allow for adjustment and adaptability. Other examples of secondary groups assuming primary group roles are easy to find in the sports world, especially with reference to athletic teams. It is wise for the educator to note that there are assets in such function assumption, but there are also many liabilities and these must be taken into account along with the assets.

OUTCOMES. The secondary group adds a breadth to the individual which can help him in his adjustment patterns. As the secondary group increases in quantity and importance in American society, it is apparent that certain functions will have to be met by secondary groups which were formerly met by primary groups. For example, sex education has become a school-oriented rather than a family-oriented function. Driver education has passed to the schools from the peer group or the family. Religious training is church-directed rather than home-directed. As the primary group gives up its responsibilities and functions (usually quite willingly), it is to be assumed that the secondary group will acquire new functions, thus changing the internal societal structure to a great degree.

Secondary groups include the casual groupings of crowds who have face-to-face contact but no organization, and of audiences and publics which have special interests and rapport and can be guided and even manipulated. Because secondary groups do not offer strict control, they represent a potential danger as well as a great value.

GROUP BEHAVIOR AND PERSONALITY

Groups have behavior patterns which reflect the behavioral commitments of their members, but they are not necessarily identical to those of the members. One need only watch and listen to a group of sailors driving by in a bus to understand that the group has fostered a behavioral pattern which may not be the individual pattern of a single young man on the bus. Teams can act in ways that a player cannot, nations can behave by means that a statesman cannot. The group assumes its own identity and this structures the behavior and personality of the group.

tasks

Under the majority of circumstances, social behavior consists of operations that must be done by the group. The task is usually a group effort, although commitment to it is most often an individual matter. Thus, no one man plays a basketball game by himself. It takes the entire team, although ultimately it is one man who scores each basket at any given time throughout the contest. But the game depends upon the team and even the spectacular ability of one man cannot create the game. The team has to create the game, in spite of the fact that its success can depend upon individual ability.

sentiments

Groups also possess sentiments. The feelings of the group are based in its identification of task and method. Loyalty is an identified sentiment of a group. The belonging and togetherness of the group supports patterns of interdependence and interreliance. There is pride in group achievement, sorrow and concern about group misfortunes, and these all combine in forming a group loyalty which may find its expression in the individual behavior of group members.

Groups also have the potential to both love and hate. Love often manifests itself in adoration for the leadership and hate may be found in the feeling toward other groups. There are times when these two sentiments are deliberately engendered by a society. The obvious time is when the society is threatened with regard to its very existence, such as during war. The members of the armed forces are purposely indoctrinated with love and loyalty for country and national philosophical concepts, and with hatred and indifference for the enemy and for the philosophical commitment which the enemy has.

Athletic teams utilize the same sort of indoctrination technique, but usually to a much lesser degree. Thus, the team is taught to have pride in its ability, faith in the coach, and loyalty to the organization and publics which support it. Teams are also taught to be skeptical about the opponent, to be doubting with regard to the opponent's ability, and, in some cases, to actively dislike the members of the opposite team. Pep talks and mass rallies are used as techniques for engendering group spirit and getting the point across.

The sentiments of a group can be powerful emotional forces which have the ability to change group behavior. A lynch crowd is a group whose sentiments are no longer under rational control, and the riots which occur after athletic contests may be described in the same way.

participation

One type of participation that groups foster is the participation of the group in a situation where the entire group interacts with other people, including other groups. Nationality groups interact with each other in Olympic settings. At times the situation is not conducive to fine performance and athletic excellence, but tends to be a national contest which is based upon supposed superior attributes that ostensibly are related to place of birth and the societal culture of a particular nation.

Sentiments, tasks, and participation are all mutually dependent upon each other. Homans has noted that people who give a great deal to each other get much in return and those who receive are under the strong obligation to give equally. He suggests that the "cost and value of what [one] gives and what he gets vary with the quantity of what he gives and gets" (1958, p. 606).

manipulation

Group behavior may be purposive or nonpurposive; it may be rational, nonrational, or irrational; and it can be conforming behavior, or it can be deviant behavior. Many people attempt to manipulate the behavior of the group to give additional force to their own views and goals. Such a procedure is a tricky one at best, but it has yielded significant results in terms of meaningful acts. The manipulation by a political leader of the destiny of his country is a well known maneuver. The manipulation of a family to do certain tasks and reach certain goals almost has become identified with the wife-mother role in the American culture; the manipulation by the teacher to have the class desire certain objectives is a time-honored technique of the teacher-student relationship, and the manipulation by the coach to "shape up" a team is almost standard procedure.

There is a certain amount of antagonism in current educational circles about manipulation. It is suggested that in a democratic society, the group itself should have the opportunity to guide its own destiny, set its own goals, and determine its own means. This belief has had far-reaching effects on certain aspects of developmental education. There are many teachers who believe that guidance is really subtle manipulation, and they support such a technique as the obligation of a teacher. There are other teachers who believe that their job is that of a resource person and that what guidance they give comes from intelligent understanding by the group of its selected tasks, its sentiments, and its interaction.

GROUP INTERACTION

The group interacts both within itself and with other groups and people. The internal interaction sets the temper of the group, and the total group's interaction with others brings direction and meaning to group organization.

internal interaction

As a group interacts within itself, the members take each other into account according to the structure of the group. Primary group members know that each person is an important component of the group structure, so they tend to accept each member as an individual with the knowledge that no member can ever really be replaced. In contrast, secondary group members know that people merely represent concepts and the individual value of each person is always subjected to the concept which that person supports.

It is not necessary for the members of a group to be of equal importance in order to have meaningful internal interaction take place. Interaction always depends upon communication, and the acts and perceptions of the group may be so subtle that only the initiated can understand them, or they may be so obvious that any person who is allowed to observe the group is capable of understanding.

The group usually has jokes, problems, and delights which are unique to it, and group cohesiveness and high interaction ability depend upon the rapport which is built up within the group.

Internal interaction is best established when the working lines of communication have some degree of formality, when there is no clear answer to a problem, when the communication is from equal to equal or from high to low, when the group members are in close proximity with one another, and when no one person is attempting to manipulate the group.

external interaction

Groups respond at times as a unit, and thus interact with other groups. For example, the two great political parties of the United States tend to interact with one another on frequent occasions. One university will react to another in terms of a group response, and an athletic team can react to many other people, including school administrators and alumni.

The group tends to have better judgment than any single member when the problems are technical rather than attitudinal. The group also tends to have judgment priority when no initial judgments with respect to a problem are alike, but instead there is a wide range of ideas as to problem solutions. A group's composite thinking is usually better than the opinion of any one person. If the task requires that each group member offer a judgment, the composite judgment of the group has much to offer in terms of simplicity and efficiency. The group also reacts well when its behavior is the result of additive information and skills. Sometimes the group can acquire knowledge that individuals can never amass. Group behavior, and consequent interaction, is also superior to the individual's when that task that must be done has several built-in "traps" which the individual could, in all likelihood, miss, but the group has the ability to sense.

Groups may cooperate with other groups, compete with them, or be in conflict with them. Any pattern of interaction may be the correct one for any given occasion. However, it is fairly certain, if two groups exist side by side over a period of time without external conflict, that acculturation will finally occur and the tasks, sentiments, and interactions of the groups will overlap and blend. There are many people in the United States who honestly believe that there are no basic differences between the Democratic and Republican political parties. It is almost impossible to note any differences between the American and National Baseball Leagues and, as schools assume community identification and universities assume regional identification, it may be impossible to distinguish one institution from another.

group deviance

Deviation is a normal aspect of group behavior and a natural outcome of interaction. It is not necessarily a sign of pathology. Often deviance forces a group to reestablish its equilibrium. There are also times when deviance can lead to group disorganization. This will occur with the greatest ease when the needs of the group are diminished, when the group is no longer satisfying the needs of the individuals who are its members, and when the needs of individuals are no longer satisfied by any group. Deviation brings out established patterns of interaction, just as conflict does.

GROUP LEADERSHIP

Every group is ultimately concerned with a certain degree of leadership. When people who are members of the group gain sufficient power and prestige to direct others, leadership is born. The membership usually grants the leader esteem as well as power. The group leader becomes the central figure in the web of communication within the group and with the "outside" world. Bell and Sirjamaki have pointed out that the leader in any group must have a "zone of indifference," (1965) a range of actions where the followers will accept the leader's judgment without question and where the leader feels enough security or personal effectiveness that he does not fear group reprisal for his actions. This is the leader's working capital.

Leaders reflect the norms of a group and are chosen because they appear to be able to affect the group's means of goal attainment. The leader's proficiency emerges as he sponsors and pushes those things in which he has specific talents. If he can convince the group that his special talents are the means to achieve group ends, his position will be assured. The best leaders have both intellectual and social ability; that is, they are able to offer ideas and they are also concerned about the welfare and image of the group, taking pains to make sure that their actions reflect both their ideas and their social concerns.

The best sort of leadership attempts to help individuals within the group achieve private goals and does not always insist that private goals be subservient to group needs. If the individual's goals can be carefully interwoven with the group's goals, so that few individuals realize that they are serving two masters, the leader will be most effective. Such organization usually is an outcome of democratic rather than authoritarian leadership.

Redl has suggested ten different types of leaders around which a group will rally (1957). He contends that each leader, in a sense, structures the group after his own ability. The leadership suggested by Redl is not inflicted leadership, but is usually elected. His leaders are the patriarchal sovereign, the group leader, the tyrant, the love object, the aggressor, the organizer, the seducer, the shepherd, the bad influence, and the good example.

patriarchal sovereign

This leader is usually a kindly, all-knowing, parent image who rules the group with a firm but loving hand and believes that his right to rule comes from the type of credentials which support his role. Thus, the teacher, the coach, and the minister often assume this traditional role. The patriarchal sovereign is often the object of admiration and respect, but he must also expect to have rebellion within his group, especially from people who desire equality. The graduate professor would have a more difficult time in this role of leadership than the undergraduate professor. The manager of the professional ball team would encounter more problems in playing the part of the patriarchical sovereign than the high school coach.

group leader

This type of leader usually emerges from the group itself and feels a real obligation to support the group in all of its endeavors. He feels responsible both to the group and for the group. His idea is to be one with the group and still not one of them. He uses his influence to steer group action, but he is also guided by group concepts and goals. He is the unusual person who can successfully sit on a fence, see both fields, and not lose his perspective.

the tyrant

This is the leader who obtains his position because he has enough information with regard to each member of the group for the group to feel that its security is in jeopardy. They then turn to the tyrant, believing that if "they can't lick him," they had better make sure that he joins them. The tyrant is usually unreasonable in his demands and sees the group as a means of serving his personal goals, which may or may not be in accord with the group goals. The tyrant is feared and perhaps even hated, but his authority and sly abilities are usually respected and honored.

the love object

Some leaders emerge from the group because they have qualities that are endorsed and loved by the group. They merely represent ideas and ideals with which the group is enamoured, although they themselves may not have the ability to lead. Such figures have the aura of leadership. The love object leader may even object to his leadership role, but usually he is overwhelmed by the accolades of love which surround him, and he is convinced in spite of his better judgment. There are times when the role creates the person, just as there are times when the person is inadequate for the role.

the aggressor

Leadership assumed by the aggressor is often seized from the group at a crucial time, usually during a time of crisis. The aggressor has energy, a certain amount of foresight, and the ability to be active and dynamic when the occasion presents itself. He also has the ability to recognize a situation which he can dominate, and he does not hesitate to "rush in where angels fear to tread." His aggression may prove to be group salvation or it may create a dictatorial complex.

the organizer

Organization is a desire common to most people, and when a person emerges with the ability to put things in logical order, he has the grounds on which to appeal to the group in its choice of leadership. The organizer always renders an important service to the welfare of the group, and this service can often be best exploited by giving the organizer the leadership role. Most organizers make effective leaders, but occasionally there is a person who is so interested in the organizational plan that he forgets what the organization is supposed to do. The obvious result of this conduct is operational efficiency and philosophical chaos.

the seducer

The person who recognizes the sentiments of the group and knows when to play upon the heartstrings often can seduce the group into accepting him as its leader. He enamours the group by persuading them that he is the object of their emotions and that he can best translate those emotions into actions that the group will support. He tends to be self-effacing and cajoling.

the shepherd

This type of leader usually has certain organizational abilities, all of which are directed toward making the group a cohesive force with strong loyalties and great pride in group endeavors. He shepherds ideas, people, and actions; he counts on his leadership being acknowledged because the herd always identifies itself with a shepherd and wants to be "taken to their leader."

the bad influence

Some groups, especially groups in rebellion against societal standards and cultural norms, will choose the bad influence as their leader, hoping through recognition of his leadership to flaunt their deviation before the society as a whole. The choice of the bad influence as a leader always carries with it an implied threat from the group to all other people with whom they interact. This choice suggests that this group is not accessible to any outside authority. The bad influence may have leadership abilities or he may be so self-centered that he is a poor leader. Groups that choose bad influences for their leader do not usually reform their leadership by virtue of the position.

the good example

When the good example is chosen as the leader of the group, the group is usually attempting to create its image through its leadership choice. The good example may not be typical of the group's personality and behavior, but more often he is the ideal of the group's wishes. Consequently, the good example is not always in touch with reality, and his leadership potential may evaporate because he talks and acts not in ways that the group understands, but only in ways that the group thinks that perhaps it should understand.

In order to remain leader of any group, no matter how the leadership was obtained, the leader must maintain his power and always think of himself as leader; he must conform to the group norms, providing original insights when called upon and being innovative enough for it to appear that he represents the frontier of the group's thinking. The leader must always give orders that he is reasonably sure will be obeyed and know what he will do if an order is disobeyed. He will give praise and scold according to the group consensus of sanction. His communication is most effective through established channels, and the good leader tries always to base his decisions on the whole situation rather than on any one aspect of a problem or on the welfare of any one member of the group. The leader creates conditions within the group so that the group will be willing to discipline its own members. Finally, he comes close to understanding himself, so that he is able to analyze his relation to the group with some degree of objectivity.

the bureaucratic leader

The bureaucratic leader always works toward group goals through individual goal attainment of the members. He makes deals to accomplish his goals in a systematic and thoughtful way, and he creates a hierarchy of authority within his group that assures group continuation if he should no longer be leader. The bureaucratic leader cares more for the group interests than he does for his own, and he is willing to play down the "I" and play up the "We."

the charismatic leader

The charismatic leader inspires the group, is unwilling to compromise principles, does not delegate authority, demands loyalty to his person and his position of leadership, and considers himself, with respect to certain group actions, as infallible. Because of his personal involvement he is often the salesman of an idea, and his "I" and "We" involvement is couched in terms "Mine" and "Ours." His loving attitude can solidify a group or make it weak. In many respects the charismatic leader is a potential threat to any group because he is so much harder to depose than the bureaucratic leader.

IMPLICATIONS FOR PHYSICAL EDUCATION

The socialization of man has a significant relationship to the fitness, movement, and play commitment of physical education. Berelson and Steiner have emphasized that "the more people associate with one another under conditions of equality, the more they come to share values and norms and the more they come to like one another" (1964, p. 327). Such an opportunity is afforded often in relation to physical education. Physical educators are constantly dealing with subcultures and groups within those subcultures. The class, the clinic, the recreational organization, the team are all important components of the organization of physical education. In addition, physical education sponsors the secret land and lingo of sport, and there is a tendency for people who form groups and subgroups to maximize their shared values.

Play groups and neighborhood recreation groups are often of a primary nature, and people find ways to effect their socialization by membership in these groups. It has been suggested by Landis that, next to the family, the most important primary group is the childhood play group (1958).

Secondary groups are also fostered by physical education activities. Teams and class groups which are secure in their identity are more tolerant of deviation than socially mobile groups. The small group influences the behavior of its members on many occasions, and the more stable and cohesive the group, the greater its behavioral influence. An athletic team has the ready-made structure to supply such a social phenonemon. Teams are relatively small and stable, and they have a common basis for their tasks, sentiments, and interactions. We know that when a person is caught in the cross pressures of different groups he will move toward his most strongly felt tie, and game and athletic groups have the potentiality to develop such strength.

Cowell, Daniels, and Kenney report that college freshmen cared as much about the social values of their physical education classes as they did about the biological values of activity (1951, pp. 286–97). There seems to be ample evidence, as reported by Cavagnaugh (1942, pp. 63–74), Annarino (1951), LaPlace (1954, pp. 313–19), and McGraw and Tolbert (1953, pp. 72–90) to support the contention that athletic ability and sports participation contribute significantly to the adjustment and adaptation process of man. Mankind tends to put a value on sports, games, movement, and fitness, and since physical education fosters these, it would appear that society should support the general idea of physical education.

Physical education activities provide communication symbols that are non-verbal in nature, and thus add to the group's opportunity to socialize its members. Also, physical education activities provide opportunities for interaction within groups and interaction between groups. Such interaction gives leadership the opportunity to rise within the group and, although physical education has no premium on the type of leadership that it sponsors, there does seem to be an unusual opportunity for the emergence of the group leader and only few opportunities for the emergence of some of the less desirable forms of leadership.

Physical education has the unique opportunity to organize an adolescent subculture and give it direction through an activity program. As the primary groups appear to dissolve, it is well that certain secondary groups in education be equipped to take over primary function even though it might not be the most desirable way to make sure that primary group tasks are accomplished.

Physical education provides one of the tasks that a group may undertake to give its organization meaning. Historical sentiments surround sports and games, and societies endorse fitness as a national attribute. If the group's task involves learning to move in a meaningful way, the group interacts as it learns through movement symbols.

Man forms social groups to help with his cultural assimilation and his socialization, and as one identifies with his team, he also identifies the role that he will play in life and the type of interaction that will give purpose to his living. Groups and teams are important, and the discipline of physical education cares about the team concept.

V

Social
Stratification

"Who ya' think you are, anyway?"

The assertion of the American Declaration of Independence that "all men are created equal" suggests a philosophic ideal rather than a functional reality. In truth, all men are not created equal, and their lives are spent in testament to the inequities of life. In a sense, equality must be earned. The real American dream is not that people shall be equal, but that there shall be *equality of opportunity* for man to become what he can.

Inequality is manifested in many aspects of living, and it is usually such inequality which adds to the challenge of American life. Inequality can be zestful in America because we permit and encourage social mobility, which is the fundamental test of a real democracy.

All societies create a system of moral and material valuations which relate people to goals. Such a system helps to integrate the society and gives a sense of meaning, understanding, acceptance, motivation, and security to life. This system, the *stratification of society,* provides the basis for wishes and desires and is the permissive sanction for what Mercer has called "palpable ambiguity and ambivalence" (1958).

If all human positions were equal in importance, it would not make any difference as to who did what job and there would be little cause for aspiration and ambition. But, realistically, it does make a difference in our society as to who does what, for some positions need more talent than others and some are functionally more important, thus demanding recognition of worth in terms of values.

The structure of the importance, responsibility, and privileges of roles in society is seldom sanctioned, or even recognized, by the laws of the land. Such recognition and sanction is accorded through the tradition and custom of society, which acknowledges social differentiation and endorses social stratification.

These sanctions and recognitions are based upon real or imagined attributes of individuals and groups, and as such are organized into some reasonable pattern. The pattern is one of social stratification. Cuber and Kenkel suggest that social stratification may be defined as "a pattern of superimposed categories of differential privilege" (1954, p. 11). Lundberg, Schrag, and Larsen have said that social stratification is a "division of a population into two or more homogeneous layers, between which there are differences in privileges, restrictions, rewards, and obligations" (1963, p. 329).

Socal stratification is institutionalized social inequality. It is a product of social interaction, and in its creation and subsequent recognition, it restricts interaction. Stratification is a hierarchy of values with the values being based on the cultural ideals.

In order to exist, social stratification must be accepted by the members of the society, although it can be superimposed upon them without their willingness or awareness. Stratification can be inherited, it can exist without understanding, but its existence must be acknowledged.

Because of stratification, some people get more goods, services, rewards, power, and emotional gratifications than others. Stratification is always viewed by the individual from his own role and stratum, and so status has a very subjective interpretation in any society. Barber states that "the system of stratification in any society is functionally integrative to the extent that it is an expression of some common set of values" (1957, p. 9). Social stratification in America, or any other democratic group, is a positive value and not a curse. Bereleson and Steiner suggest that "stratification is the hierarchy that is based on the respect, expressed in both action and speech, that individuals grant to one another in accordance with their conformity to the ideal" (1964, p. 453).

Stratification has been the product of geographic conditions, of past heritage, of the "hero concept," of feudal systems, and of certain philosophic commitments. Merrill believes that the factors that influenced the social stratification system of the United States were: the closing of the frontier and the curtailment of immigration, both of which influenced drastically the stabilization of American society and fostered the assumption of individual and group roles, which, in turn, created status, and with status came stratification; the increased fertility of the upper classes, who started to reproduce themselves instead of counting on interclass mobility to swell their ranks; the concentration of corporate control, which expanded the business interests of the society and gave more people management opportunities; and the evolution of ethnic barriers which was a partial consequence of voluntary and enforced immigration. In addition, Merrill suggests that the break in skill hierarchy, with the advent of industrialization, and the role of education have both made meaningful contributions to the changes that have been fostered in social stratification.

Basically, the functions of stratification are those of simplification, motivation, and coordination. Simplification helps with the organizational pattern of society, and motivation and coordination assure that role assumption will be possible in the future as well as the present.

All societies are stratified to some extent, and the bases of stratification are numerous. Usually, ranking is according to authority, power, ownership, consumption, education, income, occupation, kinship, divinity, morality, altruism, religion, ethnic status, association, and organization ties. Each society chooses those factors which best reflect the "ideal" of the society and ascribes to these theoretical traits a value. The nearer people or groups approach the ideal, the higher their rank in the stratification hierarchy. The further away from the ideal people are, the lower their rank.

Stratification can encourage people to want to "move ahead" or it can keep people "in their place." It depends upon the type of stratification utilized. Stratification is always dependent upon the status accord of a society and it reflects such acknowledgment.

STATUS AND RANK

Social status is a position of general prestige which is relative to other members of a group and is accorded to an individual or a group by the interacting members. Status is based upon the recognition of others that there is a claim of difference which is based on what Talcott Parsons (1940, pp. 841–61 has called *qualities, performances, possessions,* and, most important of all, whatever the peers conceive the role of status to be. Qualities are certain descriptive attributes of a role, performances are the attainment of a quality which always involves a process of change, and possessions are the exclusive rights to an idea or thing which can be either inherited or obtained through performance. Status is cumulative and is always qualified as high or low, implying the values "superior" and "inferior." With status goes responsibility, privilege, immunities, and obligations. When status is shared by members of a group we speak of group status. Thus an athletic team has status that may be different from the status of any member of the team although each member reflects the status of the entire team.

When two status groups interact, the interaction may be along a continuum from segregation of each group with virtually no interaction to integration between groups with maximum interaction. The distance which separates people and groups of different status is called *social distance,* and it is possible to measure the amount of social distance between two status roles.

As long as there is no interaction between status roles—that is, as long as there is segregation—there are no problems. There are many people who believe that the only way to world peace is to avoid interaction because a lack of interaction results in a paucity of problems. But fortunately, or unfortunately, the world is not that simple, and the proximity of people and ideas makes interaction, and hence problems, inevitable. If all status roles were of equal value, the chance of friction would be considerably less than it is. But social status and status groups are not equal, and it is the inequities of social status that is at the bottom of most rebellion and revolution.

status in America

Americans like to think that they belong to a classless society with basic equality being the constitutional right of each citizen. However, this American assumption is far from true, for the United States is a society where there are multiple status symbols, multiple status groups, and multiple interpretations of status roles. There is not even equality of opportunity for status in America, much as we like to believe that there is; for opportunity is always limited by the character of the social structure and the interpretation of what sort of opportunity should be afforded people of different status.

Status in the United States has not been linked to kinship quite as much as in other societies. There are some people who argue that the only real status determinant is related to wealth. However, the facts argue against both of these assumptions, for status in the United States reflects the kaleidoscopic view of culture which this society possesses.

The status groups in America are groups of people who have a style of life common to all members of the group, especially with respect to standards of manners, residence, general consumption, and recreation. Such a group often develops persistent prestige symbols with regard to dress, speech, mannerisms, and behavior.

Americans usually subscribe to the idea that "more means better," so superior status is afforded to the people who have more possessions, more qualities, and who exercise many performances.

It is possible for an American to have various levels of status within many groups, but when all of his status symbols are grouped together, he usually emerges with a general status identification which reflects his more important roles to a greater extent than it reflects his composite self. Wealth, power, residence, and education are important factors in ascertaining status in the United States.

status assets

Status creates its own rewards. The obvious reward—the preferential treatment in sustenance and comfort afforded the groups with high status— is readily discernible. The status concept also provides for self-respect and makes opportunities for ego-expansion. Because high, or superior, status affords expanded opportunity, there is a continual trend in the direction of status change, moving from low to high. Such mobility undergirds the American dream that anyone can be anything that he wishes to be.

status liabilities

The status of an individual usually establishes his opportunity, and his chances in life of being what he wants to be are strongly governed by his status pattern. Thus, the chances of a person having the opportunity to play professional football are infinitely better if he has played for a college team than if he has not. Therefore, college attendance, which requires both financial and intelligence attributes, becomes a necessary adjunct to the opportunity to play professional football. Such prerequisites do not always make sense, but they exist.

Status assignment tends to hold people back, as well as motivate them to move forward. There is a great deal of evidence to suggest that people who have low status often become resigned to their place in society and feel that there is no way for them to move out of the rank to which they have been assigned—an assignment which is often circumstantial. Usually the talent to fill functionally important positions is recruited from a small minority of the total potential of talent, and this minority often represents the right people who were in the right place at the right time. Obviously, many potentially fine athletes never have a chance to make their mark because they were not at the right place at the right time, and thus were denied the opportunity. Status often determines that opportunity.

Status desire is linked with unrest and anxiety, and people who have high levels of aspiration are often people who are essentially dissatisfied and disquieted. Such unrest can breed societal unrest and disruption as well as social mobility.

TYPES OF STRATIFICATION

Societies identify the sort of stratification that they use by assigning characteristics to their social order. The forms of social stratification are usually identified as *caste, estate,* and *open class.* Each of these forms is related to the others, yet each has unique features which distinguish it from the others.

caste

A caste is a closed or nearly closed aggregation. There is little movement in and out of caste, and when such movement occurs either it is done through subterfuge, or it is revoluntionary in character and has flamboyant characteristics. Caste insists that there shall be little or no intermarriage between groups. Often a caste system is characterized by the fact that the members of each caste have certain visible differences in appearance and therefore acquire certain symbolic distinctions.

One of the classic examples of caste was found in India in former years, where the "untouchables" were completely segregated within a cultural pattern. Caste has also been identified with the American Negro, although most sociologists and social anthropologists have felt that American Negro society has never been completely closed, and so technically could not be described as true caste.

There is mounting evidence to suggest that within the next half century, all caste stratification as it exists today will be eliminated. Caste denies the individual his human rights, and any civilization which professes interest in the individual cannot subscribe to caste.

estate

Estate is a type of society, a subculture, which has rights, privileges, and responsibilities according to rank within the estate. There are laws which govern the status roles within estates. The feudal system was an example of an estate, and life within a university represents a pseudo-estate form of social stratification. Students, faculty, and administration all have fairly lucid roles, and each has certain responsibilities toward the others and toward the system itself.

open class

MacIver (1937, p. 78) defined class as "any portion of a community which is marked off from the rest, not by limitations arising out of language, locality, function, or specialization, but primarily by a sense of social distance." In an open class there are no legal barriers to prohibit social mobility, and movement in and out of an open class is expected and even encouraged. In general, American society is one of open class, with class being based on status roles which are affiliated with occupation, income, place of residence, religion, education, and social reputation.

TYPES OF CLASS. Class may be defined as formally recognized by a society. An example of defined class would be "the professional class," in which the members must have a job which has been classified as professional by virtue of the education required and the credentials produced. Class may be *cultural*. A cultural class is a subculture with its own patterns of behavior and its own sanctions—for example, the adolescent society. Class may be *economic*. Economic class is exemplified by the working class as opposed to the management class. Class can be *political*, as suggested by the existence of liberal and conservative classes. Class can be *participation-oriented*, an example of which would be athletes as opposed to nonathletes. Finally, class may be *self-identified*, such as the "brain trust" of a university or the "four hundred" of a community.

CLASS IDENTIFICATION. It has been very difficult to identify class within an open society. Class is based on a complicated continuum which has no clear lines of demarcation. The two classic ways that class has been identified are in terms of Centers' ranking (1949) which is a four-item continuum consisting of upper, middle, working, and lower classes, and the six-item continuum proposed by Warner and his associates (1942) which consists of upper-upper, lower-upper, upper-middle, lower-middle, upper-lower, and lower-lower. Centers' classification depends on the self-classification of those being defined, while Warner's classification depends on a number of significant items which can be ascertained by observation and measurement, as well as judgment.

Centers injected the working-class item into his continuum when he realized that almost 95 per cent of the population in an open society tended to identify themselves with the middle class.

Warner identifies his upper-upper-class people as those who have inherited wealth and who have secure social prestige. The lower-upper class is composed of those people who have recently acquired wealth and have a less secure social background. The upper-middle-class people are the leading professional people with assured status in the society. The lower-middle people are the "white-collar workers" who have high status within the laboring society and who represent respectability and decorum. The upper-lower group of people consists of the hard working laborer—the "blue collar worker." The lower-lower group of people is composed, mainly, of the chronic misfits of the society.

CLASS DIFFERENCES. In both systems of class identification, the upper class represents wealth and security, the middle class represents respectability and stability, and the lower class represents insecurity, deprivation, and a powerless group personality.

Both the middle and lower classes have certain degrees of status anxiety and tend to have greater mobility than the upper class. The upper-class person is not as anxious about status and demonstrates limited mobility, since he has nowhere to go with regard to status. The upper-class member will seek popularity or social recognition to meet the demands of ego-satisfaction.

The lower class has a greater degree of pessimism than the middle and upper classes. The lower-class person tends to blame others for his mistakes, feels that people are not to be trusted, and possesses a greater degree of prejudice.

The behavioral differences among the classes may be found in the sex behavior of the members, the child-rearing practices, the types of communication used, the consumer expenditures, the social participation, the family decision-making patterns, the family structure, and the personality organization.

The lower-class person tends to be more promiscuous sexually than the middle class, but not necessarily more so than the upper class. Social participation in secondary groups is much lower for the lower class. There is an indication that upper-class people tend to be subject to neurosis while lower-class people tend to suffer from psychosis.

Classes differ markedly in their use of leisure, and physical educators should be cognizant of the sort of program which is offered groups of people in terms of their stratification. For example, to teach squash to a group of middle- and lower-class students would be foolish, for squash would be of little function to such a group. The teaching of squash to such a stratified group would have to be justified on grounds other than "worthy use of leisure time."

PROBLEMS. The intelligent observer of social stratification always attempts to decide if he should stay within the cultural boundaries of the stratification system, or if he should encourage class mobility. The federal government has taken the position that social mobility is desirable, and thus has initiated programs which will foster such mobility. The programs dealing with poverty adjustment and educational opportunities represent government interest in the opportunity for the population to achieve social mobility. Such responsibility, while it is questioned by a number of people, is in accord with the American dream of equal opportunity.

Social mobility brings with it a number of disturbing elements, and it is not to be expected that the change in people who are "upward bound" will occur in a decade, or even a quarter of a century. The intelligent educator will be cognizant of the implications of such programs for mobility, and will prepare facilities, equipment, and instruction to be ready in the next decade for a large influx of middle-class people with dreams that are commensurate with their newfound stratification.

PROBLEM GROUPS

Social stratification always provides lows as well as highs. Often the lows, in an open society, rebel against their status and attempt to change it. If the change is difficult, because of certain overt characteristics of the group, it is probable that discrimination may exist. Discrimination can be *approved* by a society, it can be *contested* by the society, or it can be *declared illegal* by the society. For discrimination to exist, there has to be an observable difference between people and there has to be a societal attitude toward that difference which has a certain amount of support. In the United States the problem groups could be classified as those which are concerned with race, sex, and age.

racial problems

There are no real differences that determine race. Traditionally, the races have been divided into the Caucasian, the Negroid, and the Mongoloid. Although anthropologists are divided as to whether or not true races ever really existed, it does seem apparent that at this time in the world's history there are no absolute symbols of identification which distinguish one race from another—if indeed there are races at all. "Racial" differentiation usually has been made with reference to skin color, although no more inaccurate distinction could have been chosen as identification. The coloring of all people ranges from pure white through tans and yellows to pure black, and within any group of people all colors can be found. However, in spite of the preponderance of evidence which suggests that "racial" differences are cultural rather than physical, the myth remains that races can be determined. Within certain societies, there is status accorded "race." The minority "race" almost always has the lower status, and whenever the minority threatens to become the majority, there is trouble.

In the United States there have been problems with the Orientals on the west coast, with the Mexican Caucasians and Negroes in the southwest, with the Indian Caucasians in the west and parts of the south, with the Jewish Caucasians in the northeast, and with the Negroes throughout the country, with special intensification of the problem in the south. It is evident that there is a basic inconsistency of discrimination identification. Often discrimination does not even have "racial" overtones, although we usually ascribe such a title to the objects of our discriminatory practices.

Of special concern, during the last decade, has been the discriminatory practices which have been utilized with reference to the Negro. In this case, approved discrimination became contested discrimination and then rather rapidly became illegal discrimination. The rapidity of such social change has left in its wake a certain social chaos which will probably take several generations to resolve. While it is true that the Negroes in America have waited for over a century to be granted the "inalienable" rights that they were guaranteed by constitutional edict, it is just as true that contested discrimination did not really manifest itself until after World War II and that illegal discrimination followed fast on the heels of that contesting. Thus, the advocates of approved discriminatory practices against the Negro have had a difficult time adjusting to a legal-cultural change which was brought about without the evolutionary buildup necessary for total acceptance.

The minority "races" in the United States have always had a certain amount of status mobility which was fostered by economic opportunity and by education.

In addition, status mobility has been provided by sports. Sports, which may be likened, in part, to entertainment, have always permitted and encouraged the minority factions to participate. This participation was only permitted on certain levels and within certain situations. Thus, many universities which had Negro members of basketball and football squads were not invited to play at southern universities where such practices were not allowed. However, it was not unusual for a southern university team to visit some place else in the country and play against a squad which had Negro players.

Probably the most singularly dramatic case of "racial" integration in the athletic world occurred when Jackie Robinson was brought up from the minor leagues to play baseball for the Brooklyn Dodgers. This "breaking of the color line" in major league baseball represented a social revolution in the thinking of many people. Robinson, quite mindful of his responsibilities, conducted himself in such a way that subsequent integration was facilitated and encouraged. His was a gargantuan contribution to the social mobility of the minority groups and was a special boost to the breakdown of accepted discrimination against the Negro. Next to education and economic opportunity, there is probably no other single aspect of living that has a better opportunity to initiate "racial" equality than sports.

sex problems

All societies make some status distinctions with regard to sexual roles. The differences between the sexes are obvious with regard to the reproductive process, but aside from that physiological function, it appears that there are greater differences within either sex than there are between the sexes. Although certain biological sex differences influence the height, weight, organic structure, body type, circulation, respiration, metabolism, and endocrine secretion, these differences have only had minor influence in determining social sex roles and subsequent status.

The sex roles of a society are often based upon work allocation, and with such classification comes status assignment. When these roles are clearly defined, the problems generated by sex role status are minor, but when the work assignments are interwoven without regard to sex, the status problems suggested by the sex roles heighten. Margaret Mead has pointed out that "the recurrent problem of civilization is to define the male role" (1949). Dr. Mead suggests that the male must have some prerogative that the female does not have, since the female prerogative in the bearing of children is an acknowledged physiological fact.

Many behavioral students have attempted to classify personality differences between the male and female. Traditionally, scholars such as Terman and Miles (1936) have pointed out that the female personality is that of compassion, sympathy, timidity, fastidiousness, aesthetic sensitivity, and greater emotion. The male personality is supposed to reflect self-assertion, aggression, hardiness, fearlessness, rough manners, and rough sentiment. Obviously, there are many examples of the reverse of those traits found within both sexes. It is difficult to generalize about personalities when roles are so diverse.

Because the American woman has legal and economic equality she has believed that she also has social equality. Such equality should bring with it equal status, but such is not the case. It must be acknowledged that in spite of the equality of social responsibility, the cultural heritage still insists that female status is lower than male status. This fact has been at the root of a great deal of unrest and disturbance in the American cultural pattern, for a social change with regard to sex role status is evolving and will have tremendous implications for the future of the society.

When we suggest to young women that they should have all of the rights, responsibilities, and privileges of their brothers, we are obliged also to explain why equal status does not accrue. Many women, puzzled and annoyed by the dichotomy of social description, have rebelled and become openly aggressive. Thus, the rise of the feminist movement. Other women have resorted to subterfuge and have found ways to achieve status through devious means. Thus, the rise of women "wearing the pants in the family," the "apron-stringed man," and "Momism."

For the women interested in the sports world, special problems have manifested themselves. The world of athletics was predominantly a male-oriented society, and when women demanded admission to that group, one of the last bastions of male prerogative disappeared. The young girl was accepted and indulged as a "tomboy" or "her Daddy's girl," but the older girl had to live with the tags of "mannish" and "rough and tough." While American society endorsed such characteristics for its men and permitted them for its preadolescent girls, it did not subscribe to them for its mature women. In addition, American males felt as though they had lost a citadel.

It seems important that sex roles be maintained in any society. A sexless society would be intolerable. However, how status is to be assigned to sex roles is the enigma of today's world. Equal status requires equal responsibility, and equal responsibility certainly implies equal privilege. It would appear that we must recognize that equal does not necessarily mean similar. Therefore, status which permits equality can evolve from different groups with different functions and different patterns.

age problems

In almost all societies, the elders have been afforded a high status within the group. Their advice has been sought, they have provided the leadership, and they have been the hallmark of societal erudition. In contrast to such a picture, the United States fosters the concept that the elders are of little consequence; in our country the high status of the elders is in eclipse.

In the United States the child is viewed as the major resource of the country and, therefore, he is treated with sympathy, cooperation, and understanding.

The adolescent is pampered and petted, since it is the societal belief that these are the last days before adulthood and responsibility, and thus adolescence is the time for the last days of freedom. The adolescent period is a long, drawn-out affair in America. There are no rites of puberty when manhood is assumed, and the ages from thirteen through twenty-one are viewed as a period of freedom, joy, and absence from economic responsibilities.

Since the adolescent is barred from the adult world, he creates his own culture. It is a culture in which he is allowed to experiment with sex, privilege, and economics, with few of the responsibilities that such experimentation suggests. It is a culture which is intriguing to the adult world because it offers the wistful dream come true of privilege without responsibility.

Probably in no other place in the world is there such fascination with the adolescent society as there is in the United States. With the increase in the number of adolescents, due to the increased birth rate, the adolescent society presents a powerful and formidable influence on the American social scene.

The latest adolescent clothes customs influence style; the financial needs of the adolescent as a consumer are catered to by numerous economic institutions; the sexual adventuring of the adolescent is encouraged through parental support of early marriage and societal support of illegitimacy and contraceptive practices. It has been suggested that the influence of the adolescent society may have dire consequences for the total American scene and that the nation needs to regain its perspective with regard to age. The "teenage society" is one of high status in spite of the approved and contested discriminatory practices in effect against it.

The adult age group in America is one that has all of the operations of the society within its function. The adult has status because he is the working member of society. The adult effects decisions, carries on the heritage of the race, ascertains new knowledge, and has purpose as measured by the results of his labors. The adult group is a group of responsibility as well as privilege, and its high status reflects these attributes.

It is the elder age group in America which has the lowest status. These people are no longer the major resource of the nation; they have had the opportunity to prepare for adulthood, they have already made their contribution to the function of society, and now, in their mature years, they have no purpose. Such a description has been fostered by the compulsory retirement laws of American society, by the residential pattern of families who do not live in the "old homestead" but maintain separate residences for each member of the family, and by the social endorsement of care for the elderly as a societal rather than a family responsibility.

The elders of the United States are people who have been given leisure, but have not been educated in how to spend that leisure. They are regarded as people who have already made their contribution and are therefore dispensable to the society. They are regarded as economic liabilities rather than economic assets, and their experience in living is not valued in a society which puts a premium on youth and adventuring rather than on age and wisdom.

MOBILITY

In any open society there is opportunity for mobility from one status to another. Such mobility occurs because of interaction and because the society permits the movement. Mobility is the flow, either upward or downward, between higher and lower social classes. Evidences of such mobility may be found in changes in occupational patterns, promotion within an occupational pattern, accumulation of wealth, amassing of material possessions, enrichment of educational opportunities, and assumption of social prerogatives.

America has long been enamoured with the Horatio Alger myth which suggests that upward mobility is desirable, possible, and always of positive value. Classes that achieve upward mobility usually want more opportunities for such mobility. Mobile people always tend to identify themselves with the upper level to which they aspire.

assets of upward mobility

A society which encourages upward mobility will be a richer society in terms of possessions and performances. The great bulk of the people will be in the middle class and thus will have a reasonable standard of living, which should assure something more than the minimum essentials of life. Very often the strong primary groups of a culture provide the structural support for upward mobility, and such strength in primary relationships adds to the visible strength of the society.

liabilities of upward mobility

There is a psychological strain which results from the persistent drive for upward mobility, and hence for what might be interpreted, culturally, as success. American society has been described as a departing-arriving-departing society, a rootless society with no stability. Very often personal and family disorganization may be the result of the drive to achieve. To move upward, it is often necessary to defer gratifications, and thus upward mobility may insist upon later marriage, later ownership of possessions, and later acquisition of personal qualities of status.

There is also the problem of what happens to the person who cannot achieve upward mobility and must stay where he is or even move downward. It would appear that many individuals are content to stay where they are with regard to status so long as their material possessions increase. Therefore, the dream of a car in every home, a chicken in every pot, a house for every family, and a television antenna on every roof seems to offer compensations for immobility.

The individual who moves downward is the antithesis of the American dream and is thought of as the "skidder." These individuals may be victims of *anomie,* which suggests a lack of access to achievement. The "skidder" may be so concerned about his inability to achieve upward mobility that mental illness and suicide are his only resort.

Since status in the United States is so multiple, it is quite possible that any one individual does not achieve upward mobility in all aspects of his life. A differential of status with regard to the individual's group membership is called *status inconsistency,* and it usually increases the individual's frustrations. The person who is the product of status inconsistency may be a marginal person with great social distance between his achieved status and his ascribed status. This inconsistency may be due to differentials between wealth and ethnic background, between education and wealth, between sex and education, or any number of other combinations.

Some behavioral scientists believe that social mobility is on the decline in the United States because of the emphasis upon security, tenure, and stability, rather than upon competition. However, most behavioral scientists believe that mobility is still the keystone in the arch of the American culture, and they see no reason to suspect that the keystone can be removed without the total collapse of the societal structure. Such a collapse is not foreseen.

vehicles of mobility

The two best vehicles of mobility in this country have been education and economic opportunity. As long as man can still amass a fortune and thus provide for possessions, there will be the chance for mobility and increased status in all those groups which have an economic orientation.

The use of education to increase mobility opportunity is of equal importance. Education provides certain understandings and skills which permit an individual to increase his economic opportunities as well as to enrich his cultural background. Both of these advantages enhance mobility and thus effect status change. Since both education and economic opportunity are available to many people, with minimum regard to background or finance, these are the great vehicles upon which an individual may ride as he moves from group to group and acquires new status.

In addition, sports have been used as a vehicle of mobility. Because the leisure time activities of the classes are so different, it is possible for a person of a lower class to learn the activities of a higher class and thus find status within an activity group which may, in turn, relate him to a group structured on some other principle. Thus, the Negro girl who learned tennis in the streets of Harlem was able to become a part of a tennis squad which toured the world and had access to the courts of kings. The baseball pitcher hobnobs with presidents, and the well-known and effective football coach is asked to head up a foundation sponsored by large corporate interests of industry. Such is the mobility afforded by the sports and games vehicle.

IMPLICATIONS FOR PHYSICAL EDUCATION

The movement structured by physical education which results in sports and games is both a part of the social stratification scheme of American society and a vehicle for such stratification. In addition, physical education has a stratification of its own in terms of activity importance. When infringements occur with regard to the cultural pattern of physical education activities, one naturally questions the credentials of those who promote the infringements. The answer to such questions is found in the social stratification system.

The athlete enjoys a certain high status in our society, which is related to the personality attributes ascribed to the ideal type person and group. The athlete is the aggressive conformist who personifies the "all-American" type of individual. He represents the best of the ideal and negates that which is unsavory. Because the athlete represents this perfected man, his status is high and when he falls short of the societal expectations it is more of a blow than would be the fall from glory of any nonathlete. Because of his high status, the athlete is accorded a degree of social mobility which is not available to many others. The problem groups within a society can utilize sports and games as vehicles for their own social mobility.

Within the sports and games pattern, there is also social stratification. For men, the team sports such as football, baseball, and basketball are high on the stratification scale and their adherents have a status which is accorded to all who are intimate with what are called the "major sports." The individual and dual activities are classified as "minor," and the status of the participant is correspondingly lower. The only reasonable explanation for this stratification phenomenon is in terms of the historical development of interscholastic competition. The team sports were the oldest forms of interscholastic play and have attracted more spectators and provided greater financial gains for athletic departments. All of these factors add to the accumulative effect of team sports ranking high on the stratification scale.

This stratification does not hold true with regard to women's activities. Here, the individual and dual activities tend to acquire status. The team sports still have masculine overtones in terms of cultural identification, and thus lose status with regard to women's activities. The good tennis player, golfer, or badminton player is accorded greater status than the good hockey player, softball catcher, or basketball guard.

Women athletes must be wary lest they lose status within society because of their athletic prowess. The role of the woman athlete is still not a generally endorsed role for the American girl, and status loss sometimes accompanies the decision to press hard for performance excellence.

For those people who guide the fortunes of athletic teams and individual sports talent, there is an associated status gain. Thus, the high school coach is often the most revered man in the public school system—especially if he is successful. The physical educator rises in status through association with a class that has high status accord. This makes the obligation of that person especially pressing, for the image of the social class is often looked for in its leader. Therefore, the physical educator, the coach, or the athletic director has an aura about him that pushes him to be a paragon of virtue. When he is less than that, he feels that he has failed his group as well as himself.

VI

Social
Processes

"If ya' don't like it, whatcha gonna do?"

Ideas are a part of the abstract intellect. They acquire real meaning only when they are made overt by the behavior of people. The interactions of people are governed by the social processes, and those processes which connote meaning between people are those which are significant in the socialization of man.

The social process always involves values, which have been fostered by the culture, and it is toward those values that actions are directed. The actions are structured with respect to people, who must be related to each other in some degree in order for the values to be achieved. This relationship of person to person with regard to a cultural value culminates in an actional pattern of behavior which can be defined and studied.

The social processes always insist upon adjustment of some sort. Social adjustment may be likened to the process of biological adaptation. Adjustment guarantees the equilibrium of a society in the same way that adaptation guarantees the homeostasis of the organism. Thus, as Brown has suggested, social adjustment is the "process through which the relationships between persons, groups, and culture elements are established on a mutually satisfactory basis" (1957, p. 190).

Attitudes influence social adjustment. They are nourished by the personality of the individual which in turn is sustained by the culture of the society. Thus, attitudes are a part of the culture, just as social adjustment is inherent to the culture.

Social processes are classified according to the number of people involved, the degree of intimacy between individuals, and the nature or pattern of the process.

people involved

People can be related to one another on a one-to-one basis, a one-to-two basis, a two-to-two basis, and so on. The general levels of interaction occur between individuals, between individuals and groups, between groups and the culture expectations, and between individuals and the mass media which represent the total components of a society. The relationship of a teacher to a student demands social processing, as does the relationship of a teacher to a class. The teacher must be alert to the social expectations demanded of teachers, and she must also understand the value of the subject matter.

At one time it was believed that if all of these factors were positive—that is, if the teacher and student liked each other, the teacher and student liked the class, the teacher liked to teach, the student liked being taught, the student and teacher liked the subject—an ideal educational arrangement would be in effect. However, this positive interaction no longer appears to be an accurate picture of purposeful social change, and it is felt that certain negative elements can enhance the education process.

degrees of intimacy

The intimacy of the relationship between people is reflected by the social process. There can be a *primary* degree of intimacy which involves a mutual sharing of ideas and a common will for a shared result. In a *secondary* relationship, the degree of intimacy is less reciprocal, and in a *tertiary* or *marginal* relationship the degree of intimacy is unplanned and comparatively incidental. Primary intimacy exists, for example, between two teammates or between two squads from the same educational institution. Secondary intimacy might be found between athletic opponents from different schools; and a tertiary or marginal intimacy could exist between an individual golfer and "all golfers," or between a teacher and "all teachers." Marginal intimacy usually occurs with respect to a common role.

patterns of social processes

All social interaction lies along a continuum which extends from disassociation to association. Landis(1958) has pointed out that those processes which tend to encourage disassociation are *opposition processes* and involve *conflict* and *competition*. Those processes which are disposed to encourage association are *cooperative processes* and include *accommodation* and *assimilations*. It should be noted that a continuum is a horizontal concept rather than a vertical concept. Therefore, the behavioral scientists who have suggested that human nature involves competition, which leads to conflict, which induces accommodation, which fosters assimilation, have based their rationale upon vertical ideology. Landis, on the other hand, supports horizontal ideology, in which one process does not necessarily lead to another, although all processes are interrelated.

The need for cooperation or opposition can be related to certain observable determinants. If the value which is sought is scarce, the chance of opposition processes resulting is great; while if the value is plentiful, cooperation can be expected. We might reasonably expect there to be opposition with respect to obtaining an olympic team berth, or being crowned champion of an activity; while we can foresee that cooperation would result if a country was attempting to improve its image of physical fitness or if a group decided that play helped with the acquisition of social attributes.

Cooperation will usually result if there is a kinship or degree of intimacy between the individuals interacting, and the closer the relationship, the greater the chance for cooperation. Opposition can be expected if the people involved are strangers. Therefore, a teacher has reason to suspect that the most difficult time to relate to one's students is when the school year starts. The only relationship which exists at that time is one of tradition. Cooperation toward the later part of the year would be a logical expectation, assuming that the relationship was a congenial one throughout the teaching period.

Cooperation usually results if the interacting people have reason to believe that the rewards of their group effort will be shared equally, while competition will be dominant if there is to be unequal distribution of rewards. Therefore, when a teacher structures an assignment for a cooperative venture, she must make sure that the group is given one common grade rather than individual grades to group participants. If individual grades are assigned, the chances for cooperation are reduced. Teams have often fallen apart because of the continued star billing of one member. The rewards of status and publicity must be relatively equal if one expects a cooperative venture to be effective. The coach can help with this equalization of reward by recognition and praise in ways other than through publicity.

All of the processes of social interaction may be effected through either an authoritarian or a democratic concept. Thus, cooperation can be inflicted upon a group or it can be elected by the group as a meaningful process. Game rules tend to enforce cooperation, while team strategy is often the result of a democratic acceptance of the best plan of action to achieve a desired goal. Conflict can be inflicted upon a team by a rabid administrator or it can be democratically sought, as is usually the case in any contest in which the individual voluntarily participates.

The five basic social processes can be identified as *competition, conflict, cooperation, accommodation,* and *assimilation.* Each of these is related to the others, and most social situations involve several of the processes and very seldom just one. The basic concept of sports and games seeks to utilize the entire continuum of social interaction and never just one aspect of it. Thus, sports and games do involve competition, but they also involve cooperation. Even conflict must have a cooperative base of two interacting groups who agree to have conflict. A game situation has often been compared to life itself, and the desire to participate in such an artificially constructed contrivance has been related to the desire to play the game of life within known boundaries, with known roles, known rules, and known penalties. Sport offers the individual the opportunity to test himself against unknown odds through social processes to see if he measures up to expectation or is found wanting. The responsibility of sports to the socialization process and to the understanding of the ways that process works is fundamental to an understanding of life itself.

COMPETITION

When one person or a group seeks to obtain such an objective that the greater success of that individual or group means the less success or attainment of others, opposition exists. This opposition may result in competition or conflict. Competition comes into play when norms are provided for the "fair tactics" for achieving a goal, where the losers are expected to accede to the winners with a certain amount of grace, and where failure to obey the rules may result in conflict or the invoking of sanctions.

Opposition is a universal social process, and competition is an impersonal component of opposition. Chase comments that opposition is "a figurative skyscraper of disagreements in the world today, with a fight on every floor" (1951, p. 14). Competition is an expected and normal social process and an important factor in a democratic and dynamic society—both the cause and effect of basic social change.

The Darwinian concept of the "survival of the fittest" probably emphasized the competitive aspect of social processes out of proportion to its actual importance. This concept has been accepted so generally that there are many people who believe that man's nature is essentially a competitive nature and that all other social processes indicate weakness and unnatural ways of interacting.

The American interest in victory of the weak over the strong, which probably had its roots in the pioneer tradition of attempting to defeat nature and powerful adversaries in order to survive, and, in the democratic philosophy which suggests that each man has the opportunity to be what he wishes, has also fostered the positive value of competition as a desirable social process.

It is difficult, if not impossible, to place a value judgment on any social process but, with regard to competition, it would appear that the basic responsibility of a society is to see that competition is neither eliminated nor unduly emphasized, but instead that it is directed into channels which will result in the ultimate amelioration of human relations.

characteristics of competition

Competition is always goal-oriented and always has controls. It sets up a negative interaction between competing parties, but both parties have a positive interaction with the desired goal. Competition can be conscious or unconscious, and it usually results in some means of limited communication.

Thus, we have the conscious knowledge that one is competing in a situation when he is attempting to make the team or win the contest; or the process can be unconscious such as the type of competition that goes on between student and teacher with respect to an examination, or the competitive elements found within a university system with regard to social regulations, grades, job placement, and faculty approval and endorsement.

The rules for competition may be set up by the people involved, such as the sandlot baseball team, or they may be established by an outside agency, such as the Amateur Athletic Union or the United States Field Hockey Association.

types of competition

Competition may be within the self, between self and an established norm, between persons, between a person and a group, or between two or more groups. Certain sport activities cater to delineated types of competition. For example, the competition is with self in all types of self-imposed individual play. When one throws a snowball at a tree, misses, and tries again, he has set up his own criterion for competition and attempted to meet it. All dual sports, such as tennis, badminton, and fencing, are examples of competition between two people. In sports activities it is seldom that an individual takes on an entire group, unless it be with relation to golf where the competition is not only with an established norm, par, but also with a field or group of competitors. All team sports are organized so that one group competes against another like group. Examples of specific types of competition are found in many facets of society other than sports activities. There is the child's competition for attention and the adult's competition for recognition and respect.

Competition may be either *pure* or *limited*. Pure competition is competition with minimal restrictions, such as the total struggle of the individual for status. Limited competition may be established with respect to a single facet of the individual's abilities, such as competition to win a footrace.

Competition may be *absolute* or *relative*. Absolute competition decrees that there shall be only one winner in a contest for the prize, such as the winner of the baseball game; relative competition permits many winners, as in competition for a grade point average where many people may make high and even identical averages.

Competition may be *personal* or *impersonal*. Personal competition requires face-to-face competition between individuals, such as can be seen on the bowling lanes; impersonal competition is usually between groups and does not involve face-to-face groups. Impersonal competition is found in the case of the potential draftee competing with others to make a score high enough on an examination to qualify for draft deferment, or in the competition with unknown adversaries in a telegraphic archery meet.

Competition can be *creative* or *noncreative*. If the situation is "richer" as a result of competition, we say that the competition was creative. Such might be the case after an intramural volleyball tournament. If the competition encouraged more people to play, afforded more people with the positive results which accrue from stimulating participation, then the competition was essentially creative. But if the competition depleted the resources and wasted scarce possessions for no purpose other than competitive social process, then the competition was noncreative. An example of noncreative competition would be some of the "pony league" type activities which deplete the town's leadership supply so that the one competitive event can be served.

assets of competition

When competition is established to assist a person or group in obtaining material objects and gaining nonmaterial prestige, it can be a valuable process in promoting effort and efficiency. Most people have learned to use the competitive process in order to achieve specific goals. The young mother cajoles the baby into "seeing how many bites you can eat before big brother finishes his breakfast." The preschooler is challenged to button his suit "before I count ten." The elementary school child tries to run faster than Mary and jump higher than Jimmy. The young teen-ager wants to have the "best" bike, or to "make a really good report card." The late adolescent competes with his peers with respect to driving ability, movement ability, and material possessions. The adult works in a competitive labor market and vies with his neighbors for status, prestige, and material goods. Each of these competitive relationships encourages greater effort on the part of the participant and makes for a creative society with regard to task accomplishment. There is also a subtle value in testing one's mettle against the unknown quality of another and thus gaining insight into one's abilities and talents.

liabilities of competition

Competition has the potential of being a very discouraging social process. If the participants feel so unsure of themselves with regard to accomplishment of a task that they lack self-confidence, a little competition may destroy them completely. A person cannot compete with vigor and enthusiasm unless he thinks that he has a chance to obtain his goal. Self-confidence is necessary for that belief.

Competition is also of little value when the goals are trivial or meaningless. All-out competition for possessions or prestige of little worth can destroy individuals.

Competition can sap the energy and capacity of the competitors to such a degree that they are worth little in any other situation. It is possible to wear oneself out through the competitive process. This can often be observed in members of athletic teams who have no energy left for study and other obligations.

Finally, competition may lead to false promotion of ideas and people. Just because one competes for something and wins it does not make it worthwhile. One cannot help but wonder at the worth of the numerous beauty contests to pick Miss or Mrs. Something. The competition is keen, the prestige and material assets are obvious, but the worth of the endeavor leaves something to be desired.

CONFLICT

When competition proceeds under no rules of fair play, open conflict ensues. Conflict is usually a social process which emphasizes the differences between people and minimizes their similarities. Most societies do not endorse conflict as a positive value, and hence they attempt to eliminate conflict by a system of *reciprocal expectations*. If one person's expectations are met, these in turn set up another set of expectations which can be met, and the chances for conflict diminish. All forms of conflict are products of the social setting and can be traced to societal problems. Some of these problems have little hope of resolution unless conflict is employed as a social process. There are times when it is necessary to fight for a cause.

Revolution and war are extreme examples of conflict within and between groups. Such processes are usually devastating in their effect upon the society and have a tremendous impact on the societal culture.

characteristics of conflict

Conflict is always a personal process and it always involves a conscious effort. Although overt violence does not always take place, there is a good chance that it will.

Conflict can be *total* or *partial*. Total conflict usually involves the entire society or a large portion of it, while partial conflict involves only a segment of the society or a segment of the individual's personal commitment. Therefore, it is possible to be involved in conflict against the ruling of the umpire, as is seen in basball frequently, and this is partial conflict of an individual in a specific situation. It is also possible for a person to be in conflict against "the world" and to harbor within himself total resentment against all social institutions and all socialization processes. Such people are usually society deviates.

Conflict may be *external* or *internal*. Internal conflicts exist within the group itself, as exemplified by the fist fight between two lads within a play group situation. When conflict is external, one group is against another and this can be seen in the "rumbles" and gang wars which are sometimes held between gangs.

Conflict may be *realistic* or *nonrealistic*. Realistic conflict has an end in view and there is usually an acknowledged deadline which will terminate the conflict. Industrial strikes are examples of realistic conflict. Nonrealistic conflict involves a general hatred of people and ideas which has no foreseeable end and which may continue for years, decades, and even centuries. Nonrealistic conflict is debilitating to the participants, for it utilizes energy and strength and limits initiative and innovation.

types of conflict

Conflict may be structured in relation to any aspect of society. However, the most common types of conflict within a society have been in relation to problems between labor and management, problems which concern politics and government, and problems which deal with minority groups. Each of these types of conflict is usually instigated as a result of preferential and discriminatory treatment of the involved group. The types of conflict between groups have involved property and possessions, enforcement of ideologies, and disagreement with regard to the process by which possessions are obtained. The goals in conflict are not usually direct goals, and the interacting people have negative relationships with each other.

liabilities of conflict

Conflict is the most crucial form of opposition which people can undertake. It is drastic and has seeds of finality scattered within the process. If conflict reaches a frequency and intensity whereby the entire social system is threatened, the society may be demolished. Society must set some limits to conflict in order to keep it within bounds. If there are no toleration limits, governments fall, schools close, churches are vacated, and society is decimated.

assets of conflict

Although conflict is the most radical form of interaction and is generally conceded to be an extreme social process, it does have certain assets. Conflict sets group boundaries and strengthens the group's cohesives qualities. Conflict quickly establishes the "in" and "out" groups and identifies the "we" and "they" groups. Conflict almost always insists that one take sides. It is impossible to be neutral in conflict and still be involved. The process of neutrality is itself an act of conflict.

Conflict also acts as a safety valve for society. If a minor issue can serve as the basis for conflict, there is the opportunity to make such an issue the scapegoat, thus allowing the energies of the people to be expended sufficiently so that a larger conflict is not needed or desired. The concept of the "cold war," in which groups are in conflict about minor issues often is the safety valve for a "hot war" initiation.

Conflict also has the possibility of contributing toward group stability. This is especially true when a group divided by multiple conflicts is brought together and stabilized because of a larger conflict outside the group. Every teacher knows that the best way to bring about unity within a "split" class is to give them a task to accomplish and provide conflict with another group to solidify the actions of arguing people.

Conflict may initiate other forms of interaction, and it has the potential of serving as a socializing agent. Thus, war causes groups within a nation to interact in ways that they had never before tried. War brings together labor and management for the same labor task, and the processes of cooperation and accommodation may result.

Conflict always reveals comparative strengths and thus may foster accommodation. The easily discernible example of this is found within neighborhood gangs when individuals vie for leadership positions. Once the proposed leadership has engaged in conflict, the strength of each is known by himself, by his opponent, and by the groups which both support and do not support him. Such an assessment of strength potential may forestall additional conflict. Nations use this tactic as a warning to the world that future conflict of a larger scale will be intolerable. Hence, nations engage in minor skirmishes to display their strength, hoping to deter additional conflicts which could devastate the nation.

Conflict within a group conserves the established social divisions and helps maintain the stratification system. It can also modify the power structure of a group and cause a change in the leadership. Such a change may not always be an asset to the group, but it will reflect the essential strength of the prevailing philosophy.

resolution of conflict

In order for a society to continue to function with some degree of ease, it is essential that conflict be resolved. Kurt Lewin has suggested that to resolve conflict, the group atmosphere must be changed (1948, p. 49). This change must be an attitudinal change of the entire group and not just a change for certain individuals within the group. The change in atmosphere will involve a power structure alteration, and hence the methods of leadership will alter.

Williams has made some direct and explicit suggestions as to the resolution of conflict (1947). He suggests that conflict may best be resolved if indirection rather than frontal assault is used. He further believes that if one identifies values and life activities with his opponents, then conflict can be resolved with greater facility. Activities which lead individuals to take the other group for granted will assist with the conflict resolution. There should be focus on a goal—that is, positive identification with a goal—rather than on association between opponents or on the process of conflict itself. Finally, Williams suggests that the expectation of authoritative intervention is a "quick remedy" for the reduction of intergroup tensions and thus helps to resolve conflict.

In terms of an actual situation where such tenets might be employed, let us set up a hypothetical example of two high schools who have had inter-school conflict with regard to the attainment of superiority in athletic endeavors. Such an example is commonplace, especially in situations where the close proximity of two schools threatens the prestige status of both.

If the conflict is to be resolved, it will be necessary to change the attitudes of both groups. To do so it would probably be best to work through indirection. Therefore, it would *not* be wise to call the entire school together and make an impassioned plea for better understanding. Instead it would be advantageous to identify both groups in like terms; as high school students, as part of an adolescent society, as potential college students, as people interested in the athletic contests.

Any effort that made the opponents seem similar would be helpful. Stress should be put on the idea that all the students involved are "just a group of average high school teen-agers." The need for conflict might be resolved by establishing a common task, such as a half-time demonstration for the community, a demonstration in which both schools participated.

Obviously, as a last resort, one could threaten to cancel the contest if any impropriety of conduct occurred. Such an enunciation might direct the ire of the students toward the administration rather than toward each other. Conflict is not resolved by just hoping that it goes away. It must be resolved through understanding of human behavior.

It has been pointed out by Worrell that some people choose patterns of conflict in spite of the problems engendered by such conflict (1964, pp 32–44). Most people who welcome conflict prefer realistic and partial conflict to unrealistic and total.

Conflict cannot be completely avoided in a society, nor should we want to eradicate it as a social process. We must learn to make use of its assets, minimize its liabilities, and know how to resolve it when the occasion demands.

COOPERATION

When people or groups combine their activities or work together for the attainment of a common goal, so that the greater the success of one party the greater the success of all of the others, we have the social process of cooperation. Cooley has emphasized that the "central fact of history is the gradual enlargement of social consciousness and rational cooperation" (1920, p. 113). Cooperation is essential for the group's survival because it strengthens the social cohesion of society by reducing the status anxiety of individuals.

While competition seems to spur *individuals* to greater heights, cooperation seems to be the best motivator for *groups*. There are some people who consider any attempt to regulate competition as a completely misguided endeavor to eliminate the most fundamental form of interaction. They bemoan the promotion of cooperation since they believe that it stifles free enterprise and the unrestricted scope of competition. It is their contention that such manipulation of the social processes is not in the best interests of a healthy society.

We must acknowledge that cooperation is just as much a facet of social relations as competition, and it must be regarded as of equal potential for meaningful interaction.

characteristics of cooperation

Cooperation is direct and positive and identifies both goals and people in terms of positive action. It is a goal-directed process and always involves a conscious effort on the part of the participants. Although there are certain unconscious aspects to cooperation, for the most part it is necessary to maintain a "cooperative consciousness" when relating to others. Cooperation is not necessarily the antithesis of competition; instead it is a different social process which utilizes direct identification with goals (as does competition) and a positive attitude toward those goals (as does competition); but cooperation insists upon positive relationships between people, while competition structures negative relationships.

types of cooperation

Cooperation may be *voluntary* and initiated by the individual for reasons of self-interest or altruism. Examples of such cooperation are those found in an athletic team when the cooperation of the team's members will serve the best interests of each member and the common interest of the group. Examples of cooperation fostered by altruism are found in many of the patterns and practices of courtesy which are carried on between groups. On the athletic team, helping to locate uniforms for the opponent, making sure that the material needs of the opponent are satisfied, and cooperating with your own team members so as to establish a better spirit of cooperation, all would be altruistic in nature

Cooperation may be *coercive*, induced by societal pressures or even law. Some of the cooperation found in automobile driving practices is coercive.

It is a form of cooperative behavior which often disappears when the law is removed. Coercive cooperation is frequently the directive of a leader. Sometimes the coach or team captain forces cooperation as the only logical process to attain desired goals.

Cooperation usually involves loyalty to some objective, a mutual dependence upon all members of the group, and the organization of desires. Such process results can be engendered by competition against others, by the superior power of some internal faction, and by the cooperation of an antagonist which necessitates cooperation as a resolution to the opposing desires within a group.

It is interesting to note that cooperation is necessary for really meaningful competition to take place, and, in turn, competition fosters meaningful cooperation. In many ways the two processes entertain a symbiotic relationship—each dependent upon the other and each contributing to the well-being of the other process. Sports and games utilize this symbiosis and sponsor the functional integrity of the intimacy of cooperation and competition.

assets of cooperation

Cooperation provides for individual and group accomplishment of tasks and attainment of goals. It insists upon a common purpose, devotion to which has the potential to build *esprit de corps* within a group, as well as compassion, empathy, and understanding. When cooperation is the best way to achieve goals it becomes a situational necessity, and can help individuals achieve larger goals than they would by themselves. Cooperation usually leaves an aura of well-being in its wake and is gratefully endorsed by most societies. It is a rejuvenating process rather than a debilitating one, and it represents a higher good with spiritual overtones.

liabilities of cooperation

Cooperation can foster complacency and lack of initiative. Since it is a secure process, it may deprive the individual of his commitment to the worth of goal attainment. He tends to count on the group always to take care of him, to achieve the goal, to do the task, to split the reward. Obviously, such attitudes are not necessary concomitants of cooperation, but they may be present.

Cooperation can smother the spark of interest which makes toil worthwhile. There is real apprehension on the part of many people in America that the cooperation of socialism will engulf the competition of free enterprise, and a weak nation will result. This does not have to happen if cooperation is understood and is made to be as dynamic a social process as either competition or conflict. Sometimes it is harder to get along than to participate in opposition (as any marriage partner knows), but the rewards of cooperation are manifold and worthy of pursuit.

ACCOMMODATION

The conscious or unconscious alteration and adjustment of interpersonal relations so as to avoid conflict is accommodation. Cuber has defined accommodation as "a permanent or temporary termination of rivalrous interaction, which while not necessarily settling the issue involved in the rivalry, permits the rivalrous parties to function cooperatively in at least some respects" (1947, p. 549). Accommodation permits people to work together in a cooperative way to achieve a common goal, but it does not insist that all sense of difference be submerged. It allows individuals and groups to keep status and social well-being. It is a "face-saving" process, as it allows for adaptation of behavior.

Accommodation may be effected through truce, compromise, arbitration, toleration, or subordination. Each of these techniques employs slightly different facets of the social processes, and each has a specific pattern.

Truce suggests that the two conflicting parties decide that they will suspend their conflict by effecting an agreement for a period of time. There is the implicit concept that it will be possible to "do away" with the truce at some later date, although a truce can extend for an indefinite length of time.

Compromise insists that one of the parties give way to the other on one issue, while the other party gives way on another issue. Thus, compromise is a system of "give and take" on the part of both parties involved in the conflict.

Arbitration employs the talents of a third party to help settle the conflict. The third party approaches the issue with an objectivity which neither of the two involved parties can have, and both contenders agree to abide by the decision of the judge.

Toleration is the process whereby the two conflicting parties decide to ignore each other while maintaining a "watchful eye." Thus, the differences between the two are endured by each side, but the future is circumspectly viewed.

Subordination is when the point of view of one of the parties prevails and the other party accedes to the demands. This is not usually the result of open conflict, but instead is the rational realization by one side that the other side has greater strength and that, therefore, accommodation *must* be made.

In a sense, accommodation may be thought of as "antagonistic cooperation," and there is the implied suggestion that this cooperation has been effected because of the reasonable desires of the conflicting parties. Accommodation is structured according to the comparative strengths of the antagonists and the recognition of those strengths on the part of both groups.

Accommodation can occur by isolating the antagonistic groups, by removing the issues causing conflict, or by adjusting without resolution of differences.

Games are ways in which opponents' strengths are ascertained. Most contests on the playing field have "built-in" techniques of accommodation. A tie score is a truce, the ranking or seeding of players and teams is a compromise, the referee or umpire represents an arbitrator in terms of decision-making, strategy requires toleration, and a win or loss acknowledges subordination.

ASSIMILATION

In a sense, assimilation is the ultimate form of cooperation and the most severe form of accommodation. When different groups are merged into a homogeneous unit, we can assume that assimilation has taken place. Assimilation is always a two-way process, for people have to permit themselves to be assimilated. There are times when this license occurs without conscious effort on the part of either group. Assimilation proceeds with the greatest facility when possessions which are owned by one group are desired by another group. In the acquiring of certain possessions, there is a concurrent acquisition of cultural traits and societal functions.

Assimilation may be *unilateral,* with one of the groups more dominant than the other, or it can be *bilateral,* with the assimilation process based on a fairly equal exchange of cultural patterns. America is a country which has assimilated a number of cultural traits of many other countries and has emerged with a cultural pluralism.

The greater the cultural difference between the two groups, the greater the differences in racial characteristics, the larger the ratio of newcomers to residents, and the more rapid the influx of one cultural pattern, the slower the assimilation process will be. The greater the dispersion of one culture within the other, the more rapid the assimilation process.

In a situation in which two schools have been consolidated, one might expect assimilation to be slow if the schools represented radically different groups in terms of social, financial, and racial heritage. In addition, assimilation would be slow if one school supplied a considerably larger part of the population than the other and if the consolidation happened rapidly.

In attempting to racially integrate the schools of the land, the Supreme Court displayed social wisdom in permitting this to be structured gradually, and those communities who proceeded with integrity with regard to the integration of schools were able to effect assimilation with a minimum of problems. However, those communities which took advantage of the time allowed to postpone the inevitable process were finally caught in the midst of a social dilemma that brought with it strife, conflict, revolution, and chaos.

IMPLICATIONS FOR PHYSICAL EDUCATION

The movement of people is one of the most fundamental forms of social interaction, and such movement requires the intimate relationship of people with their universe and with each other. This interaction provides a degree of intimacy which fosters specific aspects of cooperation and competition.

The morality of sport furnishes a testing ground for all of the accepted processes of interaction and structures these processes in such a way that they are acceptable to the societal standards and the cultural concept.

Games make use of both the competitive and cooperative processes, probably utilizing each process to the same extent. Although there is a tendency to emphasize the competitive aspects of sport and game, it should be acknowledged that competition cannot occur without cooperation between opponents with regard to rules and tactics, and without cooperation among teammates with regard to task and responsibility.

Almost the only culturally acceptable way to participate in approved conflict in the United States is through a sports and games program. Physical combat is permitted in such a program, and, although the conflict is governed by certain competitive standards, there is a permissiveness about physical contact which goes far beyond the usual competitive situations structured by society. All types of competition and cooperation are inherent in game situations, and games can provide a field of exploration for the social processes which, as Roger Bannister, the first man to break the four-minute mile, noted, is "larger than a chess board and just a little smaller than life itself." [1]

The director of the Max-Planck-Institut for Physiology of Behavior in Bavaria, Dr. Konrad Lorenz, has noted that sport is "a specifically human form of nonhostile combat, governed by the strictest of culturally developed rules. . . . [Sport] educates man to a conscious and responsible control of his own fighting behavior . . . [and insists on the] value of the restrictions imposed by the demands for fairness and chivalry which must be respected even in the face of the strongest aggression-eliciting stimuli." [2]

Sport can act as a safety valve for societies, just as it can provide a self-testing situation for individuals. It is a universal language of endeavor and is one of the great cultural integrators of the world. In truth, the enunciation of Arthur Wellesley, Duke of Wellington, that "the battle of Waterloo was won on the playing fields of Eton" was not just poetic rhetoric. Sports and games have the potential to both reflect and structure a society and a culture. They promote interaction, they control interaction, they structure interaction, they are the epitome of interaction.

---

[1] *Sports Illustrated,* July 4, 1966, p. 12.

[2] Konrad Lorenz, *On Aggression,* trans. Marjorie Kerr Wilson (New York: Harcourt, Brace & World, Inc., 1966), pp. 280-81.

VII

Social Change
and Control

"Who says that's the way to do it?"

The admonition of Heraclitus that "there is nothing permanent except change" seems even more valid today than it did
in the fifth century B.C. There is nothing stable about equilibrium, for to maintain balance continual adjustment and adaptation to the pressures and forces which seek to topple a structure are necessary. Equilibrium is a dynamic relationship, and
society's struggle to maintain its equilibrium is a struggle of
forces which can only be described in terms of change. The
balance of society is like the wind. There is no stability except
in terms of the ever changing social patterns. Mobility is the
most basic design of society just as it is the most fundamental
design in the individual.

SOCIAL CHANGE

Gerth and Mills have defined social change as "whatever may
happen in the course of time to the roles, the institutions, or
the orders comprising a social structure: their emergence,
growth, and decline" (1953, p. 398). As Beck has pointed out,
society is a "boundary-breaking" and a "boundary-defining"
process, and hence is continually in a state of flux (1963, pp.
229–37). Change modifies the established patterns of interaction. This modification occurs in relation to physical goods
and social relations.

Change in society occurs when an event or series of events
happens at a particular time and place in such a way as to call
for adjustment or modification so that equilibrium can be
maintained. Social change is not a monistic but a pluralistic
process. In its modification it replaces materials and ideas and
thus emerges as a relatively new structure each time it adapts.

Any given stage of cultural development is the result of the complicated interplay of numerous factors.

It is the belief of Lundberg, Schrag, and Larsen that social change is related to the amount of energy harnessed in any given society (1963). They indicate that the energy of material resources, the energy of technology, the energy of organization, and the energy of ideology all are significantly related to change, and any society which possesses an abundance of energy will have greater change and thus greater adaptation. Such adaptation results in a dynamic, mobile, mutating society and culture.

The United States is probably the most rapidly changing society that the world has ever seen. Any given individual can assume different positions within the social structure, and these positions are subject to change in terms of status and function.

Social change, enhanced by the mobility that such change demands and surrounded by the tension that such change engenders, has the potential to lead to disorganization. This disorganization is manifested in both the society and culture. Societal change is witnessed in the mutating systems of interaction among people, while cultural change is found in the vicissitude of values, ideas, and other meaningful symbolic systems.

To ascertain social change one need only note the large number of people who are engaged in activities different from those of their parents; the introduction of new techniques, new ways of making a living, changes in place of residence, innovations in ideas and social values; and the modifications in the way men seek an ultimate meaning in life.

Social change always involves a time element. The cause of the change can occur, at times, with rapidity, but the effects of such causal forces proceed with much greater deliberation.

theories of change

The causes of social change may be technological, industrial, economic, ideological, or religious. There are many behavioral scientists who believe that social change is always the effect of large impersonal factors, while others say that the core of change is the individual man. Although there have been a number of theories related to causation of social change, most of these theories are related not to material things but to functional systems.

DIVINE DETERMINATION. The theory that change is governed only by the nebulous plan of a deity is called divine determination. This theory suggests fatalistic predetermination of change. If change is patterned only on what a deity determines, there is little reason for man to attempt to effect his own world.

DEVIATION FROM THE ORIGINAL. It is the feeling of some that man has been corrupted from his original state. This corruption may have been his salvation if it proceeded in the direction of taming the "beast" in man to turn in a more "angelic" direction; or it may have been man's downfall if it contributed to modifying the essential goodness of man into a tainted potpourri of evil.

EVOLUTION. It has been the belief of some sociologists that man is evolving toward a more meaningful existence and that as individuals evolve, so societies reflect that evolution and undergo one of their own. Thus, we have moved from a social primary state to a higher condition of interaction and social consciousness.

CYCLE. The cyclic theory, promoted by Oswald Spengler, suggests that society passes through certain stages in its changing pattern. These changes are related to the stages of the maturation of man and are labeled as childhood, youth, maturity, senility, and decline. According to the cyclic theory, there can be no arresting of this process and thus societies rise and decline and are replaced by other societies which in turn rise and decline.

CHALLENGE AND RESPONSE. The challenge and response theory of social change, as suggested by Arnold Toynbee, implies that geographic and social factors offer challenges to societies and that a society must respond to such a challenge. Any given society is capable of making only a limited number of responses, and it finds in its religious commitment the necessary factor to achieve social unification.

IDEATIONAL-SENSATE. Pitirim Sorokin inferred that things change because it is their nature to change and that such change proceeds from the spiritual to the material. Change is linear, cyclical, and irregular, and there is a determination associated with the process.

CYCLICAL-SYNCHRONOUS. Stuart Chapin and others have suggested that change is selectively accumulative. Change is also cyclical or oscillatory in character, and proceeds in the stages of growth, maturity, and decay.

TECHNOLOGICAL. There is strong current belief that all social change is directly related to certain technological changes in the societal pattern. Technological invention sponsors new processes and new products which create societal and cultural change. Thus, the steam engine has changed the history of the world, and electricity has initiated social changes that could never have occurred without it.

CULTURE CONTACT. Social change may occur as a result of the contact of people with each other. As people meet, interact, and are socially conscious of each other, there is social interplay which results in social and cultural change within a society.

SOCIAL MOVEMENTS. Change can be the result of social movements which may or may not be planned. If there is the need for a large number of people to do something about a social condition, a movement may be initiated. For example, a social movement was started in the United States with regard to the aged. In the realization that society had some responsibility toward the well-being of the aged, government instituted the social security concept, economics instituted the annuity plan, and private and public groups instituted social welfare. As a result of this social movement, social change was effected.

Most social change is brought about through individual motivation and through law.

It would appear that there is no single material or functional system which can be identified as the single cause of social change. There is a plurality in the origin of change.

kinds of social change

Change comes about as a result of either *diffusion* or *invention*. Both processes are important in assuring that there is a method for change to take place, and of paramount value with regard to social control and social planning.

DIFFUSION. The movement of a pattern of culture from one society to another or from one segment of a society to another segment of the same society is called diffusion. The cultural elements which are diffused tend to transfer from one society to another almost exclusively in terms of forms that are understood by the borrowing society. Thus, borrowing societies copy patterns of behavior as they understand them, making no attempt to understand the pattern's original culture context.

Social isolation guarantees that cultural diffusion will *not* occur and has the potential of breeding cultural stagnation. Therefore, mobility of a society is one of the ways to insure social change and thus insure social growth. In a school situation, it is obvious that diffusion can be ameliorated if the school group takes the initiative in making sure that other schools are encountered and that there is the opportunity for interaction between the groups. One of the obvious ways that this can be structured is through an interschool athletic program. Such a program is probably more important to those schools which tend to be isolated in terms of geographical location than it is to a school which is in the midst of a bustling community. Traditionally, certain private schools and certain colleges and universities have been tucked away from a broad community of relations. Interscholastic athletics is one vehicle which might be used to bring about diffusion, and thus meaningful change within individuals and the institution.

Mobility of society has been assisted greatly, as of late, by the mass media. The twist of a dial can transport people in time and space to unknown sites and eras. This encourages what can be termed *psychic mobility* and facilitates diffusion.

Material objects are more often sought as means of diffusion than cultural traits. Thus, American material possessions, such as cigarettes, synthetic articles, household appliances, and farm and building equipment, have often acted as the means for cultural diffusion. Although there are many people around the world who deeply resent the process of Americanization, there are few who are not enamoured by the material possessions of the Americans. Thus, American diffusion occurs with a minimum of deliberate planning on the part of the United States.

Diffusion does not occur like the ripple effect of a pebble thrown into a lake; instead, diffusion occurs with relation to the differentials of trade, war, intermarriage, literature, scholarship, technical knowledge, and sport. Such activities as American football, baseball, and basketball have played an important role in the Americanization pattern of cultural diffusion. Every G.I. who taught a small child of another country that three strikes make an out in baseball acted as a culture bearer for the United States and unknowingly contributed to the social change brought about through diffusion.

Diffusion depends upon the simplicity of the trait, the prestige associated with the bearers of the trait, a spirit of change in the receiving culture, contact and the social atmosphere of that contact, the status aspect of the contact, and the geographical basis of the contact. Noting these factors, it is easy to see why diffusion occurred with such ease in Japan after World War II. Such material possessions as chewing gum, such social processes as games, such cultural traits as opportunity without regard to sex, all presented an image of America to the Japanese which seemed appealing; especially when this was combined with the prestige of the culture bearers and the relationship of the two societies in terms of social atmosphere.

It is exceedingly difficult to isolate culture traits as belonging distinctively to any one society. Linton has estimated that about 90 per cent of America's culture traits were borrowed from other societies (1936). Such was certainly the case with respect to the early understandings of physical education in this country. The gymnastics concepts were borrowed from Germany, Sweden, and Denmark; the therapeutic aspects had their early beginnings in China; the games concept came from Britain; and the movement expression idea had much of its origin in France. The adherents of each of these schools of thought had strong cultural leanings as well as rational educational commitments, so it is no wonder that the late part of the nineteenth century and the early part of the twentieth century saw great confusion with regard to what was being structured as the "new physical education" in a supposedly American pattern.

INVENTION.   When there is a combination of two or more existing culture traits into something different that is greater than the sum of its parts and serves a new purpose, we say that invention has taken place. The sources of invention always come from the existing culture and its stock of ideas from what Merrill has called the "non-artificial elements" in the experience of the inventor (1965). These elements are a product of the individual genius of the gifted and unique individual.

Invention can occur with reference to any aspect of society. There can be invention with regard to aesthetics, philosophy, technology, education, sport, and medicine. The larger the cultural base from which the individual can draw, the more inventions will occur in any given society. Thus, to think of new things, one must be familiar with many things.

Although the role of the individual inventor cannot be minimized, inventions are seldom the products of the genius of only one man at this stage of the world's history. The "team" approach is the accepted method of effecting change through invention. The development of the vaccines for poliomyelitis was the result of the efforts of a number of people, each of whom made a significant contribution to the ultimate discovery of the vaccine.

The space program has been the team invention of both antagonistic and cooperative societies; no one man could have carried on a program which has invented a means of mobility to extend our world into space itself. The social inventions of international understanding which was fostered by the

League of Nations, and of the New Deal during the 1930s in the United States, were motivated and inspired by individuals such as Woodrow Wilson and Franklin Roosevelt, but they were the products of the inventive processes of many thinkers.

We cannot ignore the fact that invention can also occur as the result of a happy chance of accidents. The process is one of *serendipity,* where something new comes out of the fortuitous sequence of events and the accidental relationship of materials.

Certain social conditions favor invention. The *wisdom* of the society provides a favorable disposition to the inventive process. The more one knows, the easier it is to invent. Large populations which foster a *division of labor* encourage the inventive process. The creative energy needed for invention necessitates that the inventor be spared the tasks which involve the maintenance of his personal welfare. Invention is motivated by *rewards,* and if the rewards reflect the high status values of the society, the invention has additional incentive. Although it is true that necessity does foster invention, it should also be noted that the *appropriate techniques* for such invention must be available. Thus, although there is great necessity for inventions which will control certain health problems, the techniques for such invention are still not available, and we must wait upon cancer cures, arthritis control, and solutions to aging problems until such time as correct and applicable techniques are available to properly motivated inventors.

Invention is never an isolated process, for it always has a *derivative effect.* The invention of the automobile affected industry, government, family, and religion. The derivative effects of such social inventions as the United Nations are difficult to pinpoint because they have been so encompassing. Certainly, the original concept of Olympic competition was far-reaching in its effect, and the present concept of Olympic competition has derivative effects in terms of political prestige, ethnocentric behavior, cultural interaction, and financial implications.

patterns of change

Certain essential qualities are noted in the process of social change. First, there is in any society interested in its equilibrium a *frequency of change* which is the rule rather than the exception. Continual adjustment, and hence continual change, is a necessity in any dynamic society.

Secondly, there is a *sequence of change.* Change seems to influence change, with the "major flow of change from the more influential societal parts to the less influential ones" (Mott, 1965, p. 95). Change is a chain reaction which seems to occur in sequential patterns.

Very often *change is planned,* and it is seldom the haphazard and unpremeditated process that it appears to be. It is true that all of the subtle implications of change are not always anticipated, but most change, even in primitive societies, is structured and designed.

Social change is *cumulative,* so that as one change piles upon another a pattern is established which could be destroyed if any of the specific instances of change were reversed. The cumulative effect of change can be observed with regard to sexual equality in employment practices, which has been given legal sanction. If, for some unexplained reason, women were no longer allowed to receive the financial assets of the family inheritance, the entire structure of equal employment practices would crumble. In addition, there would be social problems, political problems, educational problems, and family problems accompanying such a change.

Finally, change is *normal*. Every phase of society is subject to change, and it is only when change does not occur that there exists a social problem. All societies who have prohibited change have eventually become minority groups and then uninfluential minorities, with societal necrosis as the final result.

rate of change

Societal change is, for the most part, a slow process. The pace is usually set by the fact that the gap between existing knowledge and the rate of invention is wide. There is a greater demand for invention than there is available knowledge, and it takes time for the technology to catch up with the demand. Change is also slow because, for the most part, behavior in a society is defined by the values of earlier days. These differences among technological knowledge, necessity for invention, and behavioral qualities make for what has been identified as a *cultural lag*. Ogburn has defined a cultural lag as occurring when two variables do not change at the same rate, so that there is unsatisfactory adjustment between the two (1957, pp. 167–74).

The cultural lag is fostered by the phenomenon of *conservation of personality*, a concept which suggests that individuals are interested in maintaining things as they are, in not disturbing the *status quo*. There is a cultural lag in all societies which do not encourage change, so that *societal attitude* plays an important role in the extent of the cultural lag evident. In conjunction with the maintenance of the *status quo,* there is the action of *vested interests* in making sure that change is slowed down. Finally, cultural lag is promoted by the *role of established social institutions* which have strong social sanctions, including what seems to be an unconscious conservative attitude. Social institutions reject change for fear that their sanctions will be undermined and the societal culture fragmented.

Cultural lags usually catch up with societal patterns, so that after a few years it is difficult to discern with ease where the lag had been.

There are a number of cultural lags with regard to physical education. One of them has to do with the acceptance of women into the athletic world. Societal endorsement for the woman athlete is far from an acceptable cultural pattern. There is evidence that this lag is being resolved in terms of the new organization patterns of the Division of Girls' and Women's Sports of the American Association for Health, Physical Education, and Recreation.

There is another cultural lag with regard to the place of organized athletics in the colleges and universities of the country. Some resolution will surely have to take place with regard to the "semi-professional" aspects of university teams. It is impossible to continue with the cultural notion that teams are recruited from the university students, when we all know quite well that the students who play on teams are recruited to play and then become university students.

Probably one of the more serious cultural lags in the athletic world is the one which exists between amateur and professional definitions of athletes. It is absurd to think that a person can continue with the grueling play and practice that is necessary to become a tennis champion and still find the time to earn a living doing something else in order to support his amateur playing opportunities. The problems of amateur status on the international scene are even more complex than they are in any single national society. Some countries subsidize their athletes; some countries rule that amateur status prevails if only a certain percentage of time is spent in earning money in connection with the sport; some countries rule that any money received for any activity that is even vaguely connected with the sport constitutes professional standing; and still other countries will allow their amateur athletes to compete in nothing except sanctioned amateur meets with a breach of this rule constituting professionalism. Resolution of this lag is imperative.

attitudes toward change

Social change in America, spawned by industrialization, urbanization, specialization, centralization, bureaucratization, and secularization, has fostered attitudes of acceptance and resistance. America has generally endorsed change because it has provided greater material and social satisfaction and has helped unify the country in terms of progress and commitment, and there seemed to be the need for change to fulfill what has been called "America's destiny" as a powerful and responsible nation. Resistance to change because of individual inertia, habitual lethargy, suspicion of new innovations, fear of breaks from tradition, and lack of knowledge has created cultural lags which have slowed down social change. For example, the resistance of Americans to the adoption of simplified spelling, or the resistance to the adoption of the metric system for universal measurement, or regional resistance to the adoption of national daylight savings times are all examples of resistance to change which creates cultural lags and which can both create problems and solve them.

individual responsibility

Behavioral scientists have the tendency to reify concepts such as society, group, status, interaction, and many other abstractions. Martindale has reminded us that social and cultural change is *always* the work of individuals (1962). Individuals may choose to band together to effect social change, they may see the need for social change simultaneously, they may act in unison in resisting or endorsing change, but ultimately it is individual man who must act, and it is the specially endowed man, the intellectual, who represents a strategic reference point for the study of cultural and social change. The major events in human history consist of the formation and destruction of societies and civilizations, and if we would wish to understand how such formation and destruction came about, we must look to the thinking, the action, and the planning of individual men.

Teachers should keep the individual as their point of reference, for in any given group may be the innovator, the inventor, the individual who will give direction to the destiny of human social change. When we become too concerned with the team, the team welfare, the team spirit, the team conduct, the team image, we can lose sight of the individual, and teachers are always responsible for individuals as well as groups. Both the star and the dud contribute significantly to the team's action, and they contribute as individuals.

SOCIAL CONTROL

Once social order is established, life moves in a more or less orderly fashion. When social definitions are questioned, then difficulty ensues. Therefore, it becomes necessary for a society to establish ways in which social controls can be set up.

The best social control is usually done through the primary group relationship with its system of sanctions; however, as society becomes more complex, the burden of social control shifts from the informal primary groups to the more formal secondary groups.

Control in the United States has started to shift from the family to the school, from the school to the government, from the family to the church, from the play group to organized recreation agencies.

Since societal consensus does not come easily in America, the control patterns differ significantly from group to group and the sanctions are diverse. Such diversity leads to confusion and a nebulous definition of acceptable conduct. Control through secondary group relations is difficult.

Social control is always afforded by *support* which allows for the control to be effected, by *permissiveness* which understands why the control is necessary, and by *restriction* which prohibits reciprocal processes and imposes stops. Without these basic premises, control can only be effected by might and physical subjugation.

There are a number of apparent examples of the shift of social control from primary to secondary groups in the United States. For instance, there is the feeling on the part of many parents that it is the school's responsibility to impose social restrictions on its students and that the family is not responsible for a student's behavior. Not too many years ago a band of mothers from the Pacific northwest were indignant because the state universities of that region did not attempt to control the alcohol drinking of the student body. It was the parents' contention that the university system had been negligent in its responsibility. When the universities requested that these same parents sign a permission slip for their children with regard to alcoholic consumption, the mothers claimed that they did not want to be put in the position of apparently not trusting their offspring or of restricting the student's social opportunities. In other words, the mothers were willing and desirous that the secondary group, the school, assume the control of the student rather than attempting to retain that control within the primary group of the family.

Other cases in point with regard to the shift of control deal with sex information and sexual restrictions. Although the family is willing to have a secondary group such as the church, school, or government draw up controls for sexual conduct, it becomes concerned when information regarding birth control and contraceptive devices is given. Thus, the family attempts to direct the secondary group. This type of indirect social control is difficult and confusing.

Physical education teachers, especially, often find themselves in the position of advising students with regard to social restrictions. The physical education teacher, because of his relationship with students, is often sought out as an advisor and confidant. This is an exceedingly difficult role to play, and the intelligent teacher must make sure that he has not exceeded his societal authority and taken over the responsibility for control which should belong to the family. On the other hand, he should be willing to offer advice and to impose sanctions at the correct time, for social control is a vital and necessary process. Rules concerning dress, conduct, and attitude are the prerogative of the school and church as well as of the family, and if the family does not wish to impose control over these aspects of societal living, then it is not amiss that the secondary group institute its own controls.

SOCIAL PLANNING

Because change is not haphazard, it is the obligation of a society to plan for its change through social action. Bell and Sirjamaki have suggested that "the purposeful development and organization of forces to bring about or accelerate changes in directions is believed desirable" (1965, p. 509). Positive societal progress is ameliorated and facilitated by social planning. Isolation and fear retard such planning. Therefore, any dynamic, democratic society must look beyond the present and make social plans for its own future.

In organizing social planning, it is necessary to determine the objectives, to develop the program to accomplish the objectives, and to involve the people affected. The federal government's interest in attempting to eliminate poverty and deprivation is a case in point. The objectives of poverty elimination have been set, a complex plan of action involving education, medicine, welfare, and finance has been structured, and the people have been involved both in the planning and execution of the social plan.

It is not to be supposed that social planning always meets with complete societal endorsement; it obviously does not. However, in a democracy it must have at least the tacit consent of the majority in order to proceed. Thus, many people are skeptical and opposed to the federal government's intervention in the status grouping of people and the financial juggling that will change that status; but the majority of the nation endorses such planning and lends its moral and physical support to the concept.

The gargantuan amount of social planning that was done in the United States in the 1930s during the presidency of Franklin D. Roosevelt is seeing its fruition a quarter of a century later in terms of a higher standard of living, financial independence, availability of educational opportunities, and land reclamation and conservation.

Physical education has responsibilities for social planning in terms of its disciplinary commitment to education. Steps need to be taken now to insure the availability of equipment, facilities, and space for the future. Planning needs to be done with regard to recreational opportunities which will be available in the future. Social planning must take into account projected numbers of people, their nature, needs, and desires, as well as the opportunity for movement experiences for all individuals within the society. Social planning in physical education must recognize the cutting edge of the discipline, the frontiers of knowledge, and must plan for the availability of physical education activity as an intergal part of the connotative and cognitive domain of man.

IMPLICATIONS FOR PHYSICAL EDUCATION

Physical education is one of the ways in which social change can be effected. It is a discipline which has not completely avoided its responsibility to inflict controls and to set boundaries for change within the province of its responsibility. When the child asks, "Who says that's the way to do it?" the physical educator, for the most part, has countered with "That's what the rule book says."

Sports and games have a special responsibility in terms of cultural diffusion, and they have been used frequently as one of the more successful bearers of cultural traits. It is to be expected that the entire concept of movement will have increasing importance with regard to social change. The emerging recognition of movement as a modality for the basic integration of man's total being will undoubtedly be reflected in terms of social control and social planning.

The cultural lags which affect physical education are products of a heritage which insists on dichotomizing man into body and mind. Such lags are, however, more a matter of time than anything else. With intelligent social planning on the part of astute physical educators, these lags should be resolved.

Social control will often fall to education, and the physical education teacher will have a major responsibility to see that such control becomes a reality. Societies usually desire control and will accept it as a part of the group identification. Physical educators should not hesitate to inflict control —it is a service rather than a duty.

As with all other teachers, it is imperative that physical educators remember that they are dealing with individuals who have great potentiality for innovation and invention. We cannot afford to lose sight of the individual in our struggle to assure significant interaction for everyone. The game must continue to be for the good of the man who plays it.

The mobility of change is acutely reflected in the mobility of man, and physical education caters to, and is responsible for, significant aspects of that mobility.

VIII

Society's
Play Heritage

"Come on over—let's play"

Man looks to work for maintenance, but it is from play that he finds sustenance. To the extent that man is nourished by play, he can find relief from the reality that is life. He can, for a time, put aside the harsh insistence of essentials and necessities and turn to the ideal construction of a world which suggests order, equity, and perfection. The sustaining quality of play consists of "that which people do when they have food, shelter, and clothing, and are rested and free from worry, when the physical compulsions of life are removed temporarily and the spirit is free to search for its own satisfaction" (Gulick, 1920, p. xii).

Play is a basic mode of behavior, an integrating thread in the design of life. It is an aspect of all societies, for the play group is the most fundamental of all peer groups. Yet, as Cozens and Strumpf have pointed out, "an examination of the works of early historians would lead the reader to believe that individuals were born and they died, they earned a living, fought in wars, and elected other individuals to political office, *but they never played!*" (1951).

Play is as old as any culture. It both reflects and directs a society's best endeavors. It is an expression of the individual and the group, and as a free expression in pursuit of a perfected ideal, it has direct and intimate concern with the questions of reality and worth. "Life is, at its highest and best—a playing of the game, a pursuing of the ideal under the rules and limiting conditions necessary for this pursuit" (1920, p. xii).

It is an enigma as to why play has been studied in such a limited fashion by the behavioral scientists. The understanding of the theories of the organization of the physical world seems like child's play compared to understanding child's play.

Yet that understanding is basic to the eventual understanding of man and his life design. Joseph Lee, the "father of the American playground movement," said that if one would wish to know what a child is, one should study his play; and if one wishes to know what a child will be, then he should direct the form of his play.

Perhaps it has been because play has been identified with childhood and immaturity that it has not commanded the respect that it deserves in terms of scholarly attention, or perhaps play is so universal and basic that it has escaped notice by hiding in the anonymity of the normalcy of its function. Yet, just as physiology has studied respiration and circulation, which are basic to the integrity of man's living, so surely it is our obligation to study play, which is basic to the integrity of man's interaction.

Caillois has pointed out that "attention has been focused upon the equipment used in games more than on their nature, characteristics, laws, instinctive basis, or the type of satisfaction that they provide" (1961, p. 57). It is the nature, characteristics, and satisfactions of play that are of real interest to mankind, for play covers a group of activities as wide as the scope of human life.

The term play comes from the Anglo-Saxon word *plegian,* a verb meaning to guarantee something, to stand up for something, to take a risk for something, to expose oneself to danger, to pledge oneself to an idea no matter the plight.

In the twentieth century, among the most significant works with regard to play are those that have been done by Luther Halsey Gulick, Joseph Lee, Johan Huizinga, and Roger Caillois.

Lee and Gulick, early leaders in the field of physical education and recreation, wrote profoundly and profusely with regard to play, but their writings apparently had little influence in the field of behavior, because they were nonscientifically oriented and because both men tended to identify their observations only with children. The works of Huizinga and Caillois, on the other hand, have attracted a great deal of attention because of the authors' positions of status within the world of the behavioral scientists and because the observations have been of an objective nature and value-free. However, one cannot help but note some of the identical and concomitant ideas that run throughout the writings of all four men. Such an inference would lend credence to the observation that empiricism is the crux of scientific theory.

It was the belief of Huizinga that play is a totality, a significant function, an irrational form of behavior (1950). He emphasized that play means something which implifies a nonmaterialistic quality in the nature of the thing itself. Huizinga believed that play was *fun* and that fun resists all analysis and logical interpretation.

Play usually has been defined by a description of its qualities. Lee suggested that play is serious, is purposeful, trains for life, is growth, and is the service of ideals (1942). Caillois has said that play is free, separate, uncertain, unproductive, governed by rules and make-believe. Huizinga believed that play was nonserious, voluntary, superfluous, free, secluded, orderly, tension producing, and secretive. Gulick believed that play was an attitude which could pervade every activity, a free expression of the self, a spirit of endeavor.

In all of these descriptions of play, there are four generalizations. In describing play, it is apparent that play is self-determined, integrated and arranged, frivolous, and discreet.

play is self-determined

Play is always engaged in as a voluntary act. The individual decides for himself if he wants to play, with whom he wants to play, by what rules he will play, and how long he will play. There are times when a person can get caught up in the spirit of fun, which is a part of play, and have this occur without conscious effort; but most of the time, play is elected. There is a need for play on the part of many people. This need is created by the diversion offered by play and by the enjoyment that play offers as temptation. Individuals seek play just as they seek the other basic elements of living, and they find therein certain needs and desires answered.

play is integrated and arranged

Play is always fixed within limits of time and space. It is governed by rules and boundaries, and the majority of the time it is an orderly process with a judge to determine rule infractions and with specific penalties enacted with regard to behavior. The course of play cannot be determined, but the goal of play is stated or understood by all of the players. Innovation is encouraged in methods to reach the final goal, but the innovations must occur within a certain latitude. Therefore, when four-year-old children decide to play "mothers and fathers," they do so in an integrated and arranged way. Decisions are made as to who will be mother and who will be father. Tasks are set as to what each person is allowed to do. Play proceeds in a certain area, such as the front porch or the back yard, and play extends over a certain period of time, such as just before lunch or right after the afternoon nap. "Mother" and "father" both have latitudes of conduct, but if they attempt to move outside those boundaries, an outside arbitrator—usually an adult—must be called.

Play which includes the organized game concept is always integrated and arranged. There are rules, boundaries, referees and umpires, a time limit, a playing field, and limitations of skill patterns which allow for only a certain amount of invention and innovation.

play is frivolous

Play is never a real-life situation, although it may imitate real life or it may have implications of real life within its makeup. Play is the most unproductive of all human behavior only because it has no cause to serve. This is not to infer that many positive behavioral patterns cannot accrue from play; they can. But play does not formulate such patterns; they are an artifact of the situation. Play never creates wealth or goods or new elements of any sort, and it always ends up with the material situation being exactly what it was before the play started. It is possible to exchange goods in the midst of play, but if play is really play, the goods exchange is seldom "for keeps," but rather just "for play." Play has no cause to serve; it is light, it possesses a touch of the flippant.

When play becomes serious, in terms of its purpose, the spirit of fun is diminished and we then have an educational process which is structured by means of a form of play behavior. In reality, classes in physical education never play in the real sense of the word. They are always playing for a reason, for an aim, for a goal, and they are always attempting to make application to real life. Not so with pure play. It has a frivolity which is untainted by morality.

play is discreet

Play creates its own world, the world of play. It is a secret world which has its own tensions, its own awareness of reality and irreality, its own concept of make-believe. It is impossible to enter the play world of another unless you are bid to enter, for if you try to enter without invitation, the play is terminated. The world of play is a different world with jokes, innuendoes, meanings all its own. The six year old plays cowboys and Indians, seeing a village of wigwams and the rolling prairies instead of the living room furniture. The tennis match is a secret world of assessing the strengths and weaknesses of opponents and teammates. There is probably no other time in life when an individual is so alive, so content, so surrounded by ideas and concepts as when he is at play. His interaction with both reality and imagination fills his very being and he has the potential to become the best of what he is.

PLAY THEORIES

There have been numerous theories as to why man wishes to play. Almost all behavioral scientists acknowledge the fact that play is a basic need, but there are numerous suggestions as to why this should be so. The play theories may be classified as they focus on recreation, energy, sublimination, imitation, life preparation, restraint, domination, wish fulfillment, and personal values.

recreation theory

This theory proposes that man "uses himself up" in his working life and that as he plays, he restores himself with additional energy, incentive, and purpose. Thus, the fatigue that is accumulated throughout the day from "on the job" work can be dispelled and eliminated by play. In addition, play restores the individual so that he is better able to meet work the next day. Obviously, such a theory has no physiological basis, but certain psychological factors of boredom alleviation may be suggested as the rationale for such a theory.

energy theory

The energy theory suggests that man is endowed with a superabundance of energy and that he must find ways to discharge this energy in an essentially wholesome pattern. Play provides such an opportunity. The adherents of this theory contend that no man can use up all of his energy in his work commitment and that play must assume the responsibility for the discharge of the overload. In this highly technological age, where labor requires a minimum work load in terms of physiological response, it does seem that physiological fatigue must be fostered in ways other than work. The energy theory of play provides the suggestion as to how this might be accomplished.

sublimation theory

In the course of his life man has many frustrations and disappointments. He is restrained by cultural pressures from reacting to these problems in the ways that are natural. He cannot strike out in anger, stamp his foot in desperation, cry in sorrow, or even cavort with joy. Play provides the opportunities to do these things, within the realm of an accepted behavior pattern; and thus play offers the opportunity to direct the energy of an impulse from its primitive aim to one that is culturally acceptable.

imitation theory

Proponents of the imitation theory of play believe that the essence of play is always mimicry and that people play as they mimic real life experiences and patterns. Thus, children always imitate activities that they have seen, and even the more structured play of adults mimics situations that are reduced from real-life size to concepts that can be handled. A chess game is a war, tag is the run and chase of life, camping is an imitation of primitive living concepts.

preparation for life theory

In this theory, it is assumed that play's main contribution is that it prepares children for real-life situations. Playing with dolls provides experiences which will prepare children for the roles of parenthood. Playing with other people will provide children with the knowledge of "give and take" needed for real-life situations. The ability to "take it" without complaint prepares the child for that same personality attribute in situations other than games and play. This preparation for life may even occur with older people, and the fact that the armed services call their training maneuvers, which simulate reality, war games, is of significance to the preparation for life theory.

restraint theory

It is believed that man is essentially an aggressive organism and that he must learn to restrain his aggressions. The proponents of the restraint theory believe that play furnishes a safety valve for the most dangerous and most indispensable types of aggression, as well as an exercise in restraint in terms of human behavior. Thus, play may act as a catharsis, educating man to the responsible and conscious control of his aggressions and fighting behavior.

domination theory

Individuals have the desire to dominate each other, and play provides the opportunity to do this within certain rules and boundaries. The desire to do better than one's fellow men is a basic desire in humans, and play encourages such a desire, but within limits. Thus, one can be better than one's opponent, one can be better than one's teammates, one can be better than some artificially contrived standard of excellence. When one succeeds in this endeavor, the desire for domination has been fulfilled and the life experience is richer.

wish fulfillment theory

Mankind has dreams that can never materialize in real life. The little girl dreams of becoming the princess, the young lad dreams of being the space hero, the adult dreams of wealth and fame. Since life parcels out such dreams only to the few, play provides the means whereby all people can have their wishes fulfilled, even if only in a secret way. Thus, the girl can play that she is the princess, the boy can play that he is the astronaut, and the adult can play at fame and wealth through games involving the acquisition of possessions, and through attaining championship status in some play category.

personal values theory

It is believed by the adherents of this theory that play enriches life and is constructed in the service of ideals. Therefore, as one plays, he adds to his living a new dimension which gives both depth and breadth to his existence and enhances his concepts of personal value and worth. Thus, play is a free expression of the self in pursuit of the ideal and always has a direct bearing on the reality and worth of an individual.

All of the above theories suggest that play must have some reason for being, and they seek to explain the reason in terms of meaningful cultural commitments. However, it is possible that play simply exists with no reason for being other than the fact that it does exist. Perhaps it need not be explained in terms of its end, but instead can be accepted in terms of its function. It exists, therefore it is.

KINDS OF PLAY

Play is a behavioral pattern of all animals. Dogs, cats, birds, horses, animals of all kinds can be seen participating in play. The rough and tumble play of two grown collie dogs is considerably different from the fire and dash of those same two dogs when they are engaged in combat. Horses chase each other and kick and rear, but their play does not resemble the intent of two hostile animals. When animals play, they seem to establish rules and boundaries by mutual accord, and they seem to understand when the limits of the rules or boundaries have been transgressed.

Man, as the most advanced animal, has more structure to his play than do other animals, for his play has psychological and sociological overtones as well as biological behavioral patterns. Man's play is usually structured so that he can overcome an opponent through some means of personal contact, so that he can conquer his environment with the tools and equipment he has accepted as a part of the contest, and so that he can communicate feeling in ways other than through written and oral language.

Play can be either *structured* or *unstructured*. Structured play has a certain organizational pattern, agreed upon by all participants, as well as a set of sanctions to enforce the correct behavior. Thus, structured play consists of games, contests, and all play forms that are directed by common consent of the participants.

Unstructured play has no such limits, for the only organization of the play lies within the understanding of the individual who is playing. Thus, the three year old can play with ten year olds, by merely running about in circles by himself in close proximity to where the ten year olds are playing tag. Unstructured play consists of kicking a can for no reason other than the fact that it feels good. To throw a rock for the sheer joy of the throw, to jump in a pile of leaves because of the ecstasy of a feeling of fall, to swing on a "monkey vine" for no reason other than the swing, to skip rope without counting, to cavort about in cartwheels and rolls because of exuberance—these are all forms of unstructured play.

Play can be symbolic in its search for identification, it can be subsistent in acquiring certain emotional and biological satisfactions, it can be sociable in relating to a group and purposefully interacting, it can be expressive in communicating self to the world. Play provides the opportunity for reflection, continuity, equality of opportunity, and acknowledgement of differences. As Burch has said, "the line between reality and unreality, work and play, is too thin and too tenuous to assume that gainfully occupied man supersedes playfully occupied man in our measures of universal human condition" (1965, pp. 604–12).

FUNCTION OF PLAY

Ultimately, play is always either a contest *for* something, or the opportunity for the representation *of* something. Play's function is to find within itself a mode of behavior which will permit these two aspects of man's needs. Consequently, we might conjecture that play's function is in its aims, even when the aims are not stated or understood. Just as it is not necessary to understand that oxygen is essential to human life in order to participate in the process of respiration; so it is not necessary to understand that play has meaning in order to play. The respiration pattern is necessary for life to progress, and the play pattern is necessary for man to behave. The essence of play, found in game behavior, is a basic part of man's makeup. Man is both a game playing and a game creating animal, and it is through play that he achieves a satisfactory sense of significance and a meaningful role in his society.

Even the community reflects the play idea, for as Long has pointed out, the community is an ecology of games (1958, pp. 251–61). The community gives structure, goals, roles, strategies, tactics, and publics to the players. As the community interacts in such situations, a systematically functional pattern of behavior results which provides for all of the social processes and forms a continuum of meaningful and purposeful actions.

PLAY PROGRESSION

There is every reason to believe that play depends upon the maturity, growth, and cultural understandings of the players. The play of children follows the order of growth, and the play of adults follows the maturity of cultural cognizance.

The play of the infant is individualistic and experimental. It consists of touching and feeling, of manipulation and construction. It is usually enhanced by the understanding of more mature individuals. When a rattle is gently shaken in the face of a baby, the child reaches out and attempts to grasp it; he then experiments with the rattle in ways that are essentially pleasing. It is tasted, sucked, thrown, and shaken. Thus the baby plays.

In the play of early childhood there is little comprehension of rules, accompanied by a desire to compete against self and others on terms set by the player. This is the age of imitation and drama, the age for experimentation with reality in terms of testing one's mettle to see if "it" can be done. Thus, the child seeks to participate in games of hide and seek, of catch and throw, of give and take. He likes a make-believe world, and in the blink of an eye can take on the personality of any hero he wishes. He seeks the company of others to enhance his play and becomes a part of the primary play group which begins to draw up rules for group behavior. It is an age that Joseph Lee has descriptively called the "Big Injun" age, where drama and skepticism are congruent.

In the play of later childhood there is regard for the rules—so much regard that rules are sometimes treated as absolutes. It is the age of belonging, of team and gang play; it seeks competition with others and with the environment, and it wants the cooperative venture of loyal and happy relationships. It is described by Joseph Lee as the Land of the Leal—the Scottish concept of well-being.

The play of adults is a continuation of the play of children, but is often structured with a purpose in mind and thus lacks the spontaneity of children's play. Because society tends to identify unstructured play with immaturity, adults' play usually has structure and super-organization. It is the result of desire, carried on with great vigor, and the only real ulterior motive of adults' play is the joy of the process. It is a time when rules are considered relative and where the socialization of man through planned interaction is an absolute.

Play usually proceeds from the simple to the complex, although there are examples of simplicity being sought as a relief from complexity. Thus, the adult may seek to play "nonthinking" games of chance to avoid the discipline of skill conditioning or deductive reasoning.

One of the interesting facets of play is that it tends to rotate with the seasons of the year. In part this rotation results from play's seeking to deal with environment. Thus, it has to be winter to have snow so that one can indulge in snow play. Summer ushers in water play.

There are many causes for the seasonal aspect of sports. The relatively leisurely pace of baseball makes it ideal for the summer, when it is often too hot for games which involve constant running. Football probably owes its season, fall and early winter, to the fact that it is best played in cooler weather, as well as to the fact that it grew to popularity in a college setting and would naturally tend to align itself with the academic calendar. Ice hockey became established as a winter sport before the days of man-made ice and so required freezing temperatures. Basketball, an indoor sport, is best suited to the winter, when many outdoor sports have to be curtailed. Field hockey and lacrosse both need field space and can use the same field, hence they are played in different seasons when space is conducive to appropriate action.

The rotation of play activities acquires a cultural description. This is so well formulated that regulations must be set up to govern "off-season" play for certain games. Most of the seasonal rotation deals with team activities. This concept of seasonal play is so well recognized that the Division of Men's Athletics of the American Association of Health, Physical Education, and Recreation has structured its organization plan according to the seasonal aspect of sports activity.

ADJUNCTS OF PLAY

Although play may not have purpose, it does have certain concomitant values which are recognized by a society. These values, which may be positive or negative, give meaning to the overall pattern of play.

physical growth and fitness

One of the recognized positive values of play is its correlation with physical growth and fitness. Many of the physiological laws point out the fact that activity is necessary to human growth, and play fosters such activity in a way that is sought rather than prescribed. It is true that such activity could be gained through other means than play behavior, but play is such a natural function that growth is ameliorated without obvious emphasis.

Organic fitness is best achieved through movement, and here again play provides the *modus operandi* for such movement. Play fosters physiological overload, which is essential to strength, endurance, cardio-respiratory integrity, and general organic fitness.

moral growth

One of the most frequently ascribed attributes of play is the development of ethical behavior and morality in terms of sportsmanship. The rules of play insist upon interaction that emphasizes fairness, equality, and loyalty. While it is true that behavior is specific to a situation, there seems to be an overall pattern of play, something larger than the individual, or even the group itself. It is a subculture of play which insists upon the recognition of something larger than oneself: the recognition of the play situation, the game. Game behavior is dictated by the cultural connotation of the play situation, and we find such terms as "sacrifice" resplendent throughout play literature.

Play is predicated upon fairness, and although there are numerous instances when this point is violated, the instances are significant because they are in violation of the accepted concept.

Play does not automatically enforce morality, but it does encourage it. Even when playing solitaire, one knows when one cheats. Free acceptance of the moral judgments of play has the potential to facilitate moral growth, especially if the meaning of the play behavior is carried beyond the unreal world of play into the actual world of reality.

democratic understanding

Play can foster any sort of organizational understandings that are relevant to the situation, but in the United States play has a tendency to be democratic, both as a reflection of the culture and as a guide to the culture. Play insists upon equal opportunity for its participants. There is freedom of choice with regard to participation, role playing, and rule acceptance. The development of a social conscience has its roots in play activity, where one finds concern for fellow man, respect for life and liberty, and tacit endorsement of the pursuit of happiness.

GAMES—A FORM OF STRUCTURED PLAY

One of the most familiar forms of play is the structured situation of a game. In some respects, it is possible to use the terms play and games almost synonymously. A game always involves play, and very often when one plays he does so in the context of a game structure. Sport, which is a specialized sort of game, makes demands of play behavior also. However, sport may violate play principles in that it can be work for the professional. Although the professional athlete may enjoy his work, he is not playing any more than the lawyer who enjoys his work plays at law or the physician who enjoys his work plays at medicine.

Sports and games have always flourished in civilizations, and not even the puritan ethic could eliminate such behavior. Sport has been considered a process of socialization, and the game structure facilitates that process.

reasons for games

Caillois suggested that games, as a special facet of play, are created for a number of reasons (1961). There is the need to prove one's superiority by challenging and overcoming an obstacle or a person. Such action may result in the defeat of a person, or the establishment of a record, both being composite items of the same process.

Games provide the hope for the favor of destiny, and the game is structured to encourage pursuit of that destiny. Thus, in all games it is generally acknowledged that there is an element of luck. Skill may be the predominant determining factor of a game, but the luck is in being at the right place at the right moment with the right skill. In games of chance the value of skill is minimal, as the game is largely structured in the favor of destiny. Even the coin toss at the beginning of a contest to ascertain team goals acknowledges such a concept.

Games provide pleasure through secrecy, make-believe, and disguise. They transport the individual from one role to another, with all of the accompanying status symbols of the wishful role. Games are accepted ways to escape from reality and to hallucinate with societal endorsement. They make bearable the scrutiny of societal demands by giving permission for secrecy.

Games provide both fear and the ways by which fear can be inspired. In the search for security and freedom from fear, some of the zest goes from life, and games provide a way in which that fear can be restored within a given time and place, under given rules. The fear of the unknown and the apprehension connected with doubt are attitudes bestowed by games. These are sought by people who are guarded and protected by their groupings in society and who have status security. Fear provides the wonder in a world so secure that safety itself is a danger to psychological well-being.

Games foster the concept of repetition and symmetry. The wondrous thing about a game is that it can be played over—not exactly in the same way that it was played the first time, but repeated nonetheless. Man seeks ways that he can have a "second chance," and a game situation permits the opportunity for such an endeavor.

Games provide for the opportunity of improvisation, invention, and selection of solution. Although there are suggested game patterns, there is no way that you can be absolutely sure that you will gain your objective each time that you play. Consequently, you have to seek different avenues to arrive at the same goal, and this type of endorsed adventuring is challenging, tantalizing, and satisfying. Such an adventure permits the solution of a mystery or a riddle.

Because games are contrived, they have appeal in a world set apart for such contrivance. They have an interest because it is fascinating to see if their structure and organization has meaning and can afford satisfactions through their function.

Games provide the opportunity to test one's self against untested odds in terms of behavioral attributes. You can see how strong you are, you can see if you can keep your balance, you can ascertain if you are more ingenious than either your opponent or the game itself. In the knowledge resulting from such a testing situation the self is conceived.

Games also insist upon conformity to rules and laws. There is no skepticism possible with game rules, for the principle underlying rule is absolute truth. The game provides the rationale for the obligation to respect rules. There is always the temptation to circumvent the rules, but once the rule has been transgressed, the game is over or a penalty must be enacted.

Finally, games provide the opportunity for what might be called the "stirring of one's soul." They provide the flights of ecstasy that accompany a skill well executed; they provide the amity in a united and dedicated team; they demand the overpowering respect for an opponent who gives his best. They set one's head spinning with panic and apprehension, and they make for a sense of well-being.

Sports and games are one of the more significant indices of the character and personality of America. They portray the genius of its people and set the stage for cultural formulation.

American sports and games

Sports and games have achieved paramount importance in the United States. This has been augmented by the increasing availability of leisure time for many Americans. Machines have taken over many of the menial and exhausting chores necessary for the maintenance of the society, freeing the people to seek ways to fill their time with what seems to offer meaning. Sports and games have been a partial answer.

The economy of the United States also has fostered sports and game interest. Sports equipment is a major product of American industry and helps support a system of free enterprise.

Sports and games have permitted America to utilize her ample outdoor resources. In a country where the climate permits a temperate living, there is great need to associate with the land and nature. The country was explored and opened up under such auspices, and sports and games make use of that heritage in their facilities.

The American concern with the people and the desire for humanistic treatment of all people has fostered some of the opportunities for games and sports in the United States. The development of the playground movement in Boston, the expansion of recreational opportunities in many of the larger cities, the establishment of parks and playground departments in urban settings have all been a result of the humanistic concern of America. The country has a cultural heritage of such concern which has been manifested in opportunities for sports and games, just as it has been manifested in other aspects of American life.

Cozens and Stumpf have pointed out that America has been interested in the sports picture for a multitude of reasons (1953). They believe that the geographical factors already mentioned helped to create the American sports picture. A temperate zone which facilitated outdoor games with the opportunity for spectating was advantageous to game development.

The energy level of Americans is high. This is due, in part, to technological advantages and, in part, to the climate. It is also due to the fact that Americans represented the adventuresome spirit of the societies which provided the initial stock of people. The energy needed to develop a new country and to open frontiers required a vigorous spirit and a zestful disposition. These characteristics have been the hallmark of the American for almost two centuries and they now find their expression in sports and games as well as in economic development.

America has been able to control its physical environment and to make sure that its people are relatively free from disease. Both of these factors have enhanced the energy level of the nation and have endorsed the opportunity for sport and games among the population.

Industrialization and urbanization have added to the sports and games pattern for America. These factors, in turn, spawned communication and transportation, which also encouraged the development of sports and games. When communication was more difficult, when transportation was relatively unavailable, when people were spread out into rural living units, and when industry was negligible, sports and games were scarce, but they proliferated as these factors changed.

Another subtle factor that has encouraged sports and games in the United States is the changing role of the church and school as sanctioning agencies. The close identification of games with schools has made games a part of the educational picture, and the church attitude that games are wholesome and desirable means of enhancing spiritual life is an attitude which has given a push in favor of a game-oriented society.

The government's concern for both the promotion and control of games has also added emphasis to the game concept in the United States. This governmental concern has been fostered by national crises such as war and economic depression, as well as by the humanitarian spirit.

The American economy, which is narrowing the gap between the rich and the poor, is another factor which Cozens and Stumpf believe has emphasized the country's interest in games. There was a time when most games were the prerogative of only the rich. The facilities could only be afforded by the wealthy, and the equipment was unobtainable. As the class system, based upon wealth, has slowly broken down, so the relationship of games and the leisure class has broken down. There is still some suggestion that wealth governs the type of game which people play, but it does not govern the opportunity to play a game.

A final influence that has promoted the games and sports picture in the United States is the changing status of women and the resulting alteration of the family role as a primary group. As the family concedes some of its responsibilities, the secondary institutions must assume these responsibilities. Play behavior in a game situation is an ideal modality for behavioral situations which require primary group interaction. Thus, as women tend to leave the home for periods of time, their absence alters family stability and fosters different means of behavioral sanction. Sports and games offer a means for new sanction to arise.

classification of games

A number of attempts have been made to classify games according to some understandable pattern. Gulick suggests that games can be classified as hunting and fighting games, domestic games involving playing house, games which involve fire play, and games which involve toy construction and ownership (1920). Lee suggests that games can best be classified according to the age level playing them (1942).

The first really comprehensive and reasonable classification of games has been done by the French sociologist Roger Caillois. Caillois has constructed a paradigm of games which is based upon both game description and game behavior. Basing his fundamental reasoning upon some of Huizinga's previous ideas, Caillois has offered one of the more interesting and useful concepts of game classification yet devised.

CAILLOIS' PARADIGM. The classification of games according to description is in four categories. They are *agon* (competition), *alea* (chance), *mimicry* (simulation), and *ilinx* (vertigo).

Agon (games of competition) is found in situations where adversaries confront one another, usually under ideal circumstances. The basis of the competition, the rivalry, usually hinges upon one quality, or at most a few qualities. Such things as speed, endurance, memory, ingenuity, and strength are examples of the qualities found within agon. Agon is exercised within defined limits, and the resulting action ends up with a winner who has bested a loser. Games involving agon imply a desire to win. They demand discipline and perseverance on the part of the players, for the victory or loss depends only on the self. If agon is transported from the world of play to the world of reality, it is corrupted and results in obsession with success to the point that the ends come to justify the means.

Alea (games of chance) is always based on a decision independent of the player. The player has no control over this decision, and his win or loss is based upon chance and fate rather than skill and technique. Victory is fashioned by destiny. Games of chance negate the will, which surrenders to fate. Alea suggests that work, patience, experience, application, and training are unimportant. If alea is corrupted, excessive superstition results, and such superstition can lead to a fatalistic acceptance of living.

Mimicry (games of simulation) exists in an imaginary universe which is peopled by illusory individuals. The player pretends that he is something other than what he is, and in order to do this he sheds his own personality and dons the cloak of another. Mimicry requires invention. The rules and boundaries of mimicry are not as hard set or as fast as the rules and boundaries of agon or alea. If mimicry is corrupted, the individual is alienated from his real self and assumes the self of his pretense. Mimicry involves deception, but it is a deception recognized by the player. When the deception is no longer recognized, corruption has taken place.

Ilinx (games of vertigo) destroys the stability of perception and attempts to inflict a state of panic on an otherwise stable personality. The games of vertigo are games which depend upon speed, daring, unsure control, and loss of balance. They are frequently associated with dizziness. The players to ilinx welcome a certain amount of disorder and destruction. They revel in "horseplay." If ilinx is corrupted, madness can result. This madness can be brought on by the use of alcohol, drugs, and chemicals.

In addition to the game descriptions in terms of agon, alea, mimicry, and ilinx, Caillois suggests that game behavior is an important facet of any game. The behavior is based on a continuum of which the extremes are *paida* and *ludus*.

Paida is considered as a spirit of improvisation and joy, utilizing sudden and capricious movement patterns which are usually provoked by a superabundance of zest, vitality, verve, and gaiety. The paida behavior is reflected in the spontaneous manifestation of play.

Ludus is a behavior of discipline. It is reflected in training, skill, and rule acceptance. It encourages conflict with an obstacle and relates to the basic desire to find interest, diversion, and pleasure in arbitrary, perpetually recurrent obstacles.

Paida is characterized by noise, agitation, and laughter, while ludus is characterized by patience, acceptance, perseverance, and discipline.

In agon, games suggesting paida might be the sandlot game of "One Ol' Cat" or a "pick-up" football match, while ludus could be found in play for a Little League championship or the football finals for the Parks and Recreation Department. Paida in alea might include tossing coins or playing poker, while ludus would be found in lotteries and horse racing. Mimicry would use games of make-believe as a form of paida and theater spectacles as ludus. Paida could be found in ilinx in "swinging statues," while water skiing and tightrope walking would suggest ludus.

In addition to the four basic game descriptions, Caillois points out that there can be subclassifications which are based on the combination of certain categories. There can be agon-alea, agon-mimicry, ilinx-alea, and ilinx-mimicry. He suggests that combinations between agon-ilinx and mimicry-alea are very difficult because of the basic contradictory elements within each pattern.

APPLICATION OF CAILLOIS' PARADIGM. Most structural game activity is based upon agon: the traditional team and individual sports which make up the bulk of competitive play are games of agon. Children tend in the direction of paida and adults move more toward ludus in playing these games, although there are elements of each of the behavior patterns in any age group.

Games of alea are often found in parlor games when the game depends on a toss of the dice or a spin of the wheel. Alea is utilized as a part of agon when the contest is started. The beginning of many games of competition depends upon the chance toss of a coin or the call of a number.

Games of mimicry are often played by the spectators of agon. They tend to identify themselves with the athletes and play the game from the sidelines, becoming "armchair quarterbacks."

Games of ilinx are found in the fairly recent fascination of Americans with the mastery of implements that structure games. Such games as water skiing, surfing, sky diving, skate boarding, and numerous other activities employ vertigo as their element of attraction. There is even some ilinx in games of agon—for example, the player who attempts to "swivel-hip" down the field, return the ball when not in balance, spin around his attacking opponent.

It is possible that the paradigm of Caillois may be related to other classification systems, and at a later date it may be possible to study the relationship of game structure to societal groupings, to financial status, and to socioeconomic factors.

GAME RESULTS

The sports opportunities in the United States offer many circumstances which result in societal advantages. Sports are a way of affording sanctioned competition and conflict within the cultural pattern. They provide an opportunity for the legitimate release of emotional tension and aggressive behavior.

Games provide an element of functional beauty, and thus make possible aesthetic appreciations for large portions of the society who might not have opportunities to see beauty in its usual art form.

Games foster ritual and ceremony in a world that has become too blasé about pomp and circumstance. It permits people to expand their own egos and their sense of destiny by being a part of ceremony.

Games offer an opportunity for hero-worship, which helps a group reaffirm its belief in itself and its ideals.

In a very real sense, sport and games are an integrating force in American democratic dedication. They make it possible to realize all of the tenets upon which a democracy is based because they reduce the situation to smaller than life size with respect to operation and larger than life size with respect to result. Human movement through play, games, and sports is the social matrix of the American society.

ADJUNCTS OF GAMES

Just as play has adjuncts, so do games. The concomitant values are both positive and negative, but they have bearing on the cultural pattern of the society.

language enrichment

The English language is inundated with idiomatic references to sport and games, which add both color and flavor to our speech. We talk of things not being "cricket," of not "hitting a man below the belt," of being a "good sport," of being "it," of noting that "that's the way the ball bounces," of "playing the game," of "team action," and hundreds of other descriptive phrases which are based on situations found in the world of games.

spectator participation

Americans have been accused by Jay B. Nash of being diseased with "spectatoritis," a condition in which games and sport are observed rather than a condition in which participation occurs. It is true that there are multitudes of spectators in American society. But this identification of self with sport through observation is more good than bad. Menninger points out that man needs to participate passively (spectate) because this provides an emotional outlet for people who feel weak or inferior or who fear retaliation (1942).

Art has its galleries for viewing the great works, music has its concert halls for listening to the genius of the great masters, and sport has its stadiums and coliseums for viewing the integrated movement patterns of individuals who are masters of human performance.

ethical and moral examples

Games harbor the potential for the display of the culture's ideal of ethical and moral behavior. When such conduct is corrupted, national scandals occur. The athlete who cheats is not tolerable in a society which idolizes its sportsmen. Most of the time, sport and games provide the ethical and moral examples of behavior which a society wants to support with respect to its cultural bias toward fair play and equality.

hero-worship

Hero-worship answers an urgent need in any society. The hero is essentially a noble man, an event-making man. The hero is regarded as a model, and his image tends to expand the individual's sense of his own capacity. Sports have always provided heroes for society.

The athletic hero must be more than a record breaker; he must, by virtue of his being, have done something that other men could not have done. He has to be larger than he really is, and he must envision himself as a man of destiny. "Heroes reaffirm the American idea of itself as a nation dedicated not to power but to ideals." [1]

There is no reason to suspect that games will not continue to supply a goodly portion of America's heroes. The star athlete is a man unlike other men, a man who has a sense of destiny and faith in his ability to structure that destiny.

social interaction

When one individual says to another, "Come on over—let's play," he is setting up the structure for the most fundamental and meaningful interaction possible. He is structuring a playing game, with all of the assets and liabilities that such social interaction suggests. It is an invitation which is universal. It knows no age limits, it has no socioeconomic limitations, it has few status overtones. It is a behavioral pattern which has no cause to serve other than its own function, yet it leaves in its wake a wealth of experiences and concomitants that have cultural value. Society's play heritage has been its pattern of sustenance and might well be its pattern of salvation.

---

[1] "On the Difficulty of being a Contemporary Hero," *Time*, June 24, 1966, pp. 32–33.

The Social Matrix

"It all depends on the strategy."

Man's mobility and man's language are his vehicles for interaction. It is possible that this bipolar approach to interaction has been part of the rationale for the historical concept of mind-body division. We know now that there is, in truth, no such dichotomous approach to the understanding of man and that, in spite of the complexity, we must attempt to understand the design of human life as a totality.

In order to move, man must be fit, and this suggests that organic integrity is an essential element of man's interaction. While there are exceptional examples of men who did not possess such integrity (effecting interaction through language alone) by far the great majority of people must depend upon *both* movement and language. Therefore, physical education's interest and concern with fitness, which demands both organic and performance integrity, is fundamental to the concept of interaction.

As man moves, and thus interacts, so he learns. The baby's movement in the direction of his desires, the child's movement as an emotional response, the adolescent's movement as a pattern of self-revelation, the adult's movement to interpret ideas and concepts are all a part of the "moving to learn" syndrome.

In order to move to learn, one must learn to move. The process is cyclic. Physical education has a special responsibility for the "learning to move" part of the cycle and has traditionally used sports, games, dance, aquatics, and self-testing activities to assist the individual in learning to move. Although it has appeared at times that the *process* of learning to move was an end in itself, this has never been the real intent of physical educators, for the "learning to move" part of the cycle only completed the orb which had "moving to learn" as its other hemisphere.

As physical education seeks to understand the behavior and interaction of mobile man, it is necessary to draw some theoretical formulations which could give direction to such understanding.

Kenyon and Loy (1966), White (1966), Cowell (1961), Cozens and Stumpf (1951), and others have suggested that the discipline of physical education must develop a sociology of it own, which might be subdisciplinary in character. In developing such a subdiscipline, it would appear that the use of middle range theory is desirable.

Middle range theory, as described by Merton (1964), involves the formulation of a relatively simple idea which links together a number of observations about the structure and function of social formation. Middle range theory is always of limited scope and not too far removed from the data of observation.

Theory, in order to be accurate, should be based upon scientifically assessed fact. However, there seems to be some merit in suggesting theory which is based upon empirical observation, *verstehen*, and reason. Such theory should not be confused with true scientific theory. However, it may serve a useful purpose in suggesting avenues of approach for further observations and inferences.

Kenyon (1966) has cautioned physical educators that in studying the social matrix of physical education one must be sure that there is value-free inquiry, that there is a workable conceptual system, and that there is a theoretical-empirical balance.

Recognizing that subjective theorizing is never value-free, and further recognizing that a workable conceptual system must await development, there still seems to be interest, if not value, in suggesting theoretical threads which could have meaning in understanding the design of the behavior and interaction of mobile man. Therefore, let us consider the discipline of physical education with relation to the cultural heritage, the cultural potential, social grouping, social status, social processes, and social control.

THE CULTURAL HERITAGE AND PHYSICAL EDUCATION

Since physical education is concerned with fitness, movement, and play, all aspects of those entities have certain cultural implications. From such a heritage it is possible to postulate the following generalizations.

play is a basic behavioral pattern

Man has played in every society of which history has been recorded. His play has been a part of his unitary self and has been self-determined, integrated and arranged, frivolous, and discrete. He has played in structured and unstructured ways, according to certain cultural directives, in order to test himself or to represent something which was important to him. Man could no more deny play than he could deny movement.

games reflect the culture

Games, as a structured form of play, always find their rationale in the cultural directives of a society. Games of combat, cooperation, competition, mimicry, chance, and vertigo all reflect the social processes and the value system of the society. Games may be borrowed from other cultural patterns, but when they are, they are interpreted with respect to the borrowing society's culture. Game theory is based upon the desired outcomes of the cultural pattern, and game organization reflects the societal organization which the culture endorses. Therefore, games in the United States reflect a culture that values aggression, independence, equality, and concern for the individual.

games help structure the culture

Although games have a tendency to reflect cultural patterns, they also help determine those patterns. The behavioral necessities for various types of games endorse culture traits. For example, the opportunity to disagree with the official in baseball gives tacit approval for disagreement with other officials in situations other than games: the policeman's reasons can be questioned and the rationale for any officially endorsed behavior is open to inquiry. Games also aid in cultural diffusion. The game of baseball has been significant in diffusing the American cultural pattern in other parts of the world and has been equally as effective in structuring the cultural pattern of the United States in terms of status, prejudice, and responsibility.

the "athletic world" is a subculture

Games and sport necessitate an organization that is unique to their purpose. They solidify a group of people with a common interest and a common task. They support their own set of folkways, mores, and taboos, and are regulated by a set of laws which is acceptable to all who participate. Within the society of the "athletic world" there is structure and the possibility for cultural transmission and cultural lag. The "athletic world" may include both players and workers who utilize play as their method of work. Both the amateur and professional athlete belong to the athletic world and function under the same cultural directive. When there is disparity between the two groups, there is confusion on the part of both the athletic world and the society which gives it support.

games are a microcosm of society

Part of the appeal of games rests upon the fact that they represent a society that is easily discernible to most people. Games require roles, tasks, and sanctions. Games have boundaries and they have a permissive attitude toward endeavor. These characteristics are discerned because they are in a situation which is structured and is small enough for comprehension. Societal structure and function is diverse and complex, but game structure and function is unitary and simple. As games relate to society, so they are a picture of society. Games are used frequently as an analogy for societal description. They are a microcosm of society.

CULTURAL POTENTIAL AND PHYSICAL EDUCATION

The personality of man, as reflected in the socialization process, is a composite of many factors within the cultural scheme. One of the significant factors is man's relationship with play, movement, and fitness.

movement and personality are related

The pattern of man's mobile behavior is related to his personality structure. It is possible to influence the personality through both types and patterns of movement. Conversely, the personality of man gives his movement strong directives. People who like strong, percussive movements may have a personality commitment in that direction, and those who seek out light, flowing patterns of movement may reflect that preference in their personality. Through the inculcation of certain types of movement organization, it may be possible to help formulate personality. The general public apparently believes that "sports make the man," for it encourages athletics, games, dance, and other specific movement behaviors to help with the structuring of the personality. Games are even used to help in formulating group personality, as when the armed forces make use of athletics to engender pride, determination, and team spirit in their personnel.

societal energy is related to fitness

In order for a society to possess energy for its defined tasks, it is necessary for each individual member of that society to have a high degree of personal fitness. This would indicate not only that organic integrity is necessary in a biological sense, but also that behavioral energy and performance energy are necessary. The better the balance of its individuals with respect to their energy generating and energy discharging abilities, the better the balance of the entire society. When deviation from this balance occurs, when there is stress within the individual, this is reflected in a society of deviates which cannot keep its balance in terms of goals and organization.

games establish defined roles

The entire organization of a game depends on the players' understanding of what their roles shall be with respect to the objectives of the game. These roles dictate the social process which is to be used. You cannot afford to have conflict on a team, nor can you permit unlimited cooperation between adversaries. Games set roles which can be understood and described. Insofar as games are a microcosm of society, game positions are a minute picture of life roles in a society. Insofar as the player is able to discern this relationship, it would appear that games could be an educational device for the understanding of role playing.

play insists upon discipline

The discipline of play suggests that there are limits and sanctions, and that neither of these can be transgressed without destroying the play concept. The permissiveness of play is found in its techniques, not in its rules and boundaries. In a society where there is an increasing absence of discipline from the primary and secondary groups, it could be that play will offer one of the last modes of teaching the meaning of discipline. No society has existed without discipline. Since play insists upon discipline, play could be a form of behavior which gains societal endorsement because it fulfills a societal function.

games offer sanctions

Game behavior is governed by rules and mores. Those behaviors which are desirable are offered endorsement through a set of sanctions which permit the game to continue and which afford enjoyment and fun. Those behaviors which are not desirable are not endorsed, and are subject to reprimand and penalty. Thus, when a rule is broken or a boundary line crossed, the reprisal is fast and sure. Penalties are inflicted to restore the equality of the situation. One of the meaningful aspects of game sanction is that it is immediate and understandable. In real life, sanctions may be nebulous and obscure, but in a game they are lucid and intelligible.

SOCIAL GROUPS AND PHYSICAL EDUCATION

The social grouping of society determines behavior and status. Physical education, which has always been cognizant of the "team concept," reinforces the organization of social groups and helps bring meaning to such organization.

the play group is a primary peer group

As a group which has face-to-face contact, intimate and prolonged association, and a fusion of individual behavior patterns into a group image, the play group qualifies as a primary group of peers. It is in the play group that sanctions without benefit of understanding are first imposed. You have to do it "the gang's way" or you are out of the group. The play group would seem to be essential in the normal development of an individual and of a society. The general age similarity within a play group carries a tremendous impact with regard to interaction among peers. The play group reflects the cultural milieu and offers the close association desired by those who have group hunger. This group assists in creating possibilities for human activity as it maintains a friendly and congenial atmosphere for its members. It insists upon conformity and is possessive. You have to be allowed "in," and you can be cast "out" for any indiscretion.

games create intra- and inter-action

In order for a game to maintain its integrity, it is essential that some sort of action takes place. This action occurs within the game itself in terms of performance and behavior, and it occurs between groups who are playing together, in terms of strategy and attitudes. Such action is a powerful force in the socialization process and can be employed to change and alter behavior. The action motif of a game helps to determine the groupings that can be used in any given situation, and such groupings lend endorsement to the concept of societal interaction.

games insist upon intimacy

The majority of games are face-to-face encounters and thus demand a physical intimacy which is a requisite of social grouping. Even those games which are played over a long distance, such as telegraphic meets, formal lotteries, and ceremonial spectaculars, insist on a psychological identification of participants. Bowlers, even if they are spectators and not players, identify with bowlers. Actors identify with actors, and collegiate athletes identify with collegiate athletes. This sort of intimacy decreases social distance and may enhance understanding, which could be reflected in societal interaction.

games create leaders

Games are fashioned in such a way that it is always possible for the skill and behavior of one person to be apparent to all who observe the game. Thus, the star is created and the dud is acknowledged. The person who stands out from the rest because of his performance and attitude may assume the leadership of the group. Games are clear in their endorsement of skill. They keep score. The sort of leader that is fashioned by the game will depend upon the integrity of the game and the group's endorsement of that image.

physical educators are innovators of behavior

Because the physical educator, whether he be trainer, coach, or teacher, is the acknowledged leader of the group (whose tasks are fitness, movement, and play), he has responsibilities and privileges with regard to human behavior. It is at his direction that team and individual behavior patterns are structured. As the accepted image of the group, the physical educator has a major responsibility to conduct himself in a way that is befitting the group. He also has to take primary responsibility for the personality development of individuals who make up the group. Anyone who shuns such a responsibility should probably ally himself with some other aspect of the social structure. If you choose to direct physical education, you must choose to direct behavior.

SOCIAL STATUS AND PHYSICAL EDUCATION

Some of the modalities used by physical education are status-creating. The emphasis that America puts on upward mobility and high status finds some manifestation in the physical education disciplinary picture.

status is achieved through athletics

There is a cultural endorsement of the athlete as a man set apart from the rest of the society by virtue of his superior qualities, performances, and possessions. Because he is acclaimed as different, and his difference has societal approval, the athlete acquires status. Athletic status is usually desirable in most social circles in the United States, although there are times when it is not endorsed. The academic intelligentsia tends to consider athletic status as an undesirable or at least unattractive attribute.

sports are vehicles of mobility

Social mobility is achieved in any open society when a person changes his role and thus changes his status. Sports and games offer such an opportunity to the individual in the United States. Since there is a tendency for games to reflect the interests and capabilities of certain social groups, it is possible to change groups by changing the kind of games in which they participate. Sports offer an entree to social groups which ordinarily might not be available. Playing tennis will gain admittance to the country club and its traditional socioeconomic group. Being an Olympic contender will facilitate association with political and industrial leaders who might have been unapproachable under other circumstances.

the athletic world is an open class

Although a number of people have claimed that the athletic world is a closed class society, there seems to be little empirical evidence to support such a claim in America. Admission to the athletic world is gained primarily through demonstration of skill. Although there are certain artifacts which may influence the ease of admission to this world, the potential for circumventing such artifacts is great. One need not be well educated to play football, one need not dress well to be accepted in the golfing circles, one need not possess wealth to play tennis, one need not have a certain ancestral heritage to play polo.

structured play caters to youth

In spite of the fact that there is a growing awakening with regard to physical education for the elderly, the physical education program is still a youth-oriented program, with emphasis on development rather than maintenance. Movement is facilitated for the young, fitness is more easily obtained with the young, play has a connotation of immaturity acceptable for the young. The elders of the society are, at best, a diversion for physical education. There is evidence that this situation is changing, but it would appear that the change, if it comes, will be slow. Cultural attitudes toward play will have to change, as will societal ideas of fitness.

athletics is male-oriented

The attributes demanded of athletics are very similar to the desirable attributes expected by society of its males. Because of this close correlation, the female athlete does not enjoy cultural approval for her endeavors. In order to excel, she must possess many of the "male-oriented" characteristics, and this colors her societal image as a woman. There are a few instances where this concept is changing. The change can be found partially with regard to aquatics and individual sports. Team sports, combative sports, and certain self-testing activities usually do not attract or even sanction female participation. The woman athlete should understand the status of her position and be able to adapt and adjust in ways that are meaningful both to her and to her society.

the athlete has hero potential

Because the athlete is "a man apart," he has the potential of becoming a hero. He must envision himself as a man of destiny in order to establish such a role. Then, having achieved hero standing, he must be willing to accept the status role that such standing has created. His will be the exemplary life, closely scrutinized by society for flaws, and widely emulated. For the individual who dislikes such typing, it would be wise to attempt to avoid endorsement as a hero.

SOCIAL PROCESSES AND PHYSICAL EDUCATION

A society uses certain patterns to carry on its interaction. These patterns, or processes, are a part, to some degree, of all societal endeavors. Physical education reflects all of the processes in a way that is easy to acknowledge. It even endorses some of the processes which many other endeavors seek to avoid—for example, physical conflict. Social processes are utilized and enhanced by physical education.

games employ all social processes

The universality of physical education method makes imperative the utilization of all forms of social interaction. Cooperation and competition are both parts of most play. Cooperation is reflected in the basic neuro-muscular cooperation which is necessary for performance and organic fitness, and in the individual-group cooperation that is necessary for interaction. Although competition has been emphasized as a major component of game activity, there is no reason to believe that this social process is used any more than any other. Accommodation occurs in both movement and play. The proper balance of each of the social processes seems to lend enchantment and intrigue to physical education activities.

games sponsor approved conflict

Games are one of the few means in society where one can engage in socially approved physical conflict. The conflict may be as intimate as physical grappling, or it may be as remote as defeating an opponent by outscoring him. The conflict endorsed for games is not always physically violent, and it does have certain limitations as to time, space, and rules of conduct. But, in spite of such limitations, game conflict provides one of the few times that an individual is allowed to strike another without fear of penalty. It permits the understanding of the meaning of conflict in a society that is oversensitive about conflict, and consequently is always attempting to resolve it or to prevent it from happening.

physical education behavior is specific

Although there is always the hope that behavioral patterns can be taught in one place and used in another, it would seem that each behavioral response is specific to the situation, the time, and the place in which it is employed. Therefore, we should not make the mistake of thinking that the development of social attributes in game situations automatically infers that such attributes will be employed other than in games. Any transfer of behavioral factors would have to be emphasized in order to be made applicable for use in other than a specific situation. Physical education does not teach a person how to be a good sport, or how to be honest, or how to be fair. All that physical education does is teach a person *about* honesty, fair play, equality, sportsmanship. The application of these behavioral traits must be made by each individual and each group, situation by situation.

SOCIAL CONTROL AND PHYSICAL EDUCATION

The ultimate desire of any student is to learn to control knowledge so that it has meaning and value. The student interested in the behavior of man is interested in social control, and physical education, as a discipline interested in the behavior and interaction of mobile man, is ultimately concerned with change and control of such phenomena.

physical education encourages diffusion and invention

The commitment of physical education is to change. Such change is encouraged through both invention and diffusion. As a part of education, physical education has a responsibility for creating new knowledge and ascertaining new relationships for society. As movement patterns change, as new meanings are found in movement, as new techniques are developed with regard to learning to move, so invention and societal change take place. Cultural diffusion is ameliorated by planned interaction opportunities for groups within the physical education aggregation. An absence of change would be unthinkable for physical education, for the discipline feeds upon it.

physical education recognizes the individual

Although physical education works through the concepts of the group and interpersonal interaction, the discipline is always cognizant of the worth and importance of the individual. Each person contributes to the whole, and each person is an entity within the whole. In our concern with group behavior and interaction, we must continue to realize that the only reference point that any educational endeavor has is that of individual man. Physical education recognizes the star, the dud, the "average" person, and finds in each person's behavior meaning for the group, meaning for the concept of interaction, and meaning for the discipline.

physical education has a share in social control

As each society seeks to impose its own controls, it is to education that a large part of the burden for such control falls. Because of the nature of physical education, and because of the sorts of people that direct physical education programs, a disproportionate part of the responsibility for social control may fall to the lot of physical education. This control will necessitate planning which is structured on the best theory available with regard to the pattern of human life. It will require an enterprising spirit on the part of physical educators, permissiveness on the part of society, and the acceptance of restrictions and prognostications. The physical educator who is willing to be tossed by the wind of society is not fulfilling his ultimate responsibility. If the cultural pattern with regard to interscholastic athletics is destructive to individuals and to the society, physical educators must take the initiative for change. We are not pawns of a societal chessboard; we have the potentiality to be the King and Queen of the game, and to direct and control the action within the province which has been delegated to us.

THE DISCERNMENT OF DESIGN

To see a pattern amid the complexity of human life is a difficult, if not impossible assignment. It can be assumed with reason that individual man always reacts as a biological entity and always reacts with as much integrity as his being pemits. We can not think without a neurological system, we cannot breathe without a respiratory system, we cannot nourish ourselves without a digestive system, we cannot count on organic maintenance without a circulatory system, we cannot behave without a muscular system. Man's power and his salvation are related to his biological design.

But, over and above power and survival, there is meaning that does not have biological perimeters. The behavior of man is more than his systemic response to stimuli. A conceptual pattern of interacting man emerges as he reacts with others and with his environment and his god. There is a human relativity that provides the pattern of human life.

Chase has suggested that sociology's major problems have to do with how present knowledge concerning man's interaction can be integrated and applied; how scientific behavioral sciences can be extended and verified to give a more dependable explanation of man's behavior; what dynamic process underlies the structure of the group; and what is the place of value judgments in the social sciences (1948). Physical education's major problems will be concomitants of such concerns. We are interested in the basic social units, in behavioral attributes, in the fundamental social processes. Our questions will have to be structured in relation to mobile man and the meaning of his movement.

One thing seems sure. Within the pattern of human life, movement is a dominant and powerful design. The social matrix of physical education is identified with the movement of man and his resultant behavior. As we find outlines to such a pattern, we will surely find that the pattern is relative to time, place, and the individual. But there is the distinct possibility that the *process* by which the pattern is created is identifiable and absolute. And if that is true, an understanding of human movement, fitness, and play will stand out as a recognizable thread in the multicolored pattern that is human life.

References

Adorno, T. W., *et al, The Authoritarian Personality,* New York: Harper & Row, Publishers, 1950.

Alderdice, Mary Ellen, "The Relationship Between Attitude Toward Physical Education and Physical Fitness Scores and Sociometric Status." Unpublished Master's Thesis, State University of Iowa, 1963.

Allport, Gordon, *Personality,* New York: Holt, Rinehart & Winston, Inc., 1937.

Anderson, Walfred A., and Frederick B. Parker, *Society: Its Organization and Operation.* Princeton, N.J.: D. Van Nostrand Co., Inc., 1964.

Angell, Robert C., *The Integration of American Society.* New York: McGraw-Hill Book Company, 1941.

Annarino, Anthony A., "The Contribution of Athletics to Social Mobility." Unpublished Master's Thesis, Purdue University, 1951.

Anthony, A. H., "Anxiety as a Function of Psychomotor and Social Behavior," *British Journal of Psychology,* 51:141–152 (May, 1960).

Arendt, Hannah, *The Human Condition.* Chicago: University of Chicago Press, 1958.

Austin, Mary C., and G. C. Thompson, "Children's Friendship Study of the Bases on Which Children Select and Reject Their Best Friends," *Journal of Educational Psychology,* 3:101–116 (February, 1948).

Bagey, Philip H., "Culture and Causes of Culture," *American Anthropologist,* 55:535–554 (October, 1953).

Bales, Robert F., *Interaction Process Analysis.* Cambridge: Addison-Wesley Publishing Co., Inc., 1950.

Barber, Bernard, *Social Stratification: A Comparative Analysis of Structure and Process.* New York: Harcourt, Brace & World, Inc., 1957.

Barnett, H. G., *Innovation: The Basis of Cultural Change.* New York: McGraw-Hill Book Company, 1953.

Barron, Milton L., *Contemporary Sociology.* New York: Dodd, Mead & Co., 1964.

Baruch, Dorothy Walter, *New Ways of Discipline.* New York: McGraw-Hill Book Company, 1949.

Barzun, Jacques, *God's Country and Mine.* Boston: Little Brown & Co., 1954.

Bass, Bernard M., *Leadership, Psychology and Organizational Behavior.* New York: Harper & Row, Publishers, 1959.

Bates, Frederick L., "A Conceptual Analysis of Group Structure," *Social Forces,* 36:103–111 (December, 1957).

Beals, Ralph L., and Harry Hoiser, *An Introduction to Anthropology.* New York: The Macmillan Company, 1953.

Beck, Kenneth, "Evolution, Function and Change", *American Sociological Review,* 28:229–237 (April, 1963).

Becker, Howard, and Alvin Boskoff, *Modern Sociological Theory in Continuity and Change.* New York: Dryden Press, 1957.

Bell, Earl Hoyt, and John Sirjamaki, *Social Foundations of Human Behavior.* New York: Harper & Row, Publishers, 1965.

Bendix, Reinhard, and Seymour Martin Lipset (eds.), *Class Status and Power: A Reader in Social Stratification.* New York: Free Press of Glencoe, Inc., 1953.

Benedict, Ruth, *Patterns of Culture.* Baltimore, Md.: Penguin Books, Inc., 1924.

Berelson, Bernard, and Gary A. Steiner, *Human Behavior: An Inventory of Scientific Findings.* New York: Harcourt, Brace & World, Inc., 1964.

Berger, Peter L., *Invitation to Sociology: A Humanistic Perspective.* Garden City, N.Y.: Anchor Books, Doubleday & Company, Inc., 1963.

Bernard, L. L., *Social Control.* New York: The Macmillan Company, 1939.

Berne, Eric, *Games People Play.* New York: Grove Press, 1964.

———, *The Structure and Dynamics of Organizations and Groups.* Philadelphia: J. B. Lippincott Co., 1963.

Bertrand, Alvin L., "The Stress-Strain Element of Social Systems: A Micro Theory of Conflict and Change," *Social Forces,* 42:1–9 (October, 1963).

Betz, Robert L., "A Comparison Between Personality Traits and Physical Fitness Tests of Males 20–60." Unpublished Master's Thesis, University of Illinois, 1956.

Biddulph, L. G., "Athletic Achievement and the Personal and Social Adjustments of High School Boys," *Research Quarterly,* 25:1–7 (March, 1954).

Bidney, David, *Theoretical Anthropology.* New York: Columbia University Press, 1953.

Bierstedt, Robert, *The Social Order: An Introduction to Sociology.* New York: McGraw-Hill Book Company, 1963.

Bloch, Herbert A., *Disorganization, Personal and Social.* New York: Alfred A. Knopf, Inc., 1952.

Bogue, Donald J., "The Quantitative Study of Social Dynamics and Social Change," *American Journal of Sociology,* 57:565–568 (May, 1952).

Bonner, Herbert, *Group Dynamics.* New York: The Ronald Press Company, 1959.

Borgatta, Edgar F., and Henry J. Meyer, *Sociological Theory.* New York: Alfred A. Knopf, Inc., 1956.

Boulding, Kenneth E., *Conflict and Defense.* New York: Harper & Row, Publishers, 1962.

Braybrooke, David, *Philosophical Problems of the Social Sciences.* New York: The Macmillan Company, 1965.

Brim, Orville Gilbert, *Sociology and the Field of Education.* New York: Russell Sage Foundation, 1958.

Britton, Joseph H., William G. Mather, and Alice Lansing, "Expectations for Older Persons in Rural Community Work and Retirement," *Geriatrics,* 16: 664–671 (December, 1961).

Brookover, Wilbur B., *A Sociology of Education.* New York: American Book Company, 1955.

Broom, Leonard, and Philip Selznick, *Sociology: A Text With Adapted Readings* (2nd ed.). Evanston, Ill.: Row, Peterson and Company, 1958; 1961.

Brown, B. Warren, *Social Groups.* Chicago: Faithorn Publishing Company, 1926.

Brown, Francis J., *Educational Sociology.* Englewood Cliffs, N.J.: Prentice-Hall, Inc., 1947.

———— *Sociology: With Application to Nursing and Health Education.* Englewood Cliffs, N.J.: Prentice-Hall, Inc., 1957.

Buckley, Walter, "Social Stratification and the Functional Theory of Social Differentiation," *American Sociological Review,* 23:369–375 (August, 1958).

Burch, William R., "The Play World of Camping: Research into the Social Meaning of Outdoor Recreation," *The American Journal of Sociology,* 70:604–612 (March, 1965).

Bury, J. B. *The Idea of Progress.* London: The Macmillan Company, 1921.

Caillois, Roger, *Man, Play, and Games.* Translated by Meyer Barash. New York:. Free Press of Glencoe, Inc., 1961.

Cameron, William Bruce, *Informal Sociology.* New York: Random House, 1963.

Cantril, Hadley. *The Psychology of Social Movements.* New York: John Wiley & Sons, Inc., 1935.

Cartwright, Dorwin, and Alvin F. Zander (eds.), *Group Dynamics: Research and Theory.* Evanston, Ill.: Row, Peterson and Company, 1953.

Case, Clarence, *Social Progress and Human Progress.* New York: Harcourt, Brace & World, Inc., 1931.

Cavagnaugh, Jean O., "The Relation of Recreation to Personality Adjustment," *Journal of Social Psychology,* 15:63–74 (February, 1942).

Centers, Richard, *The Psychology of Social Classes.* Princeton, N.J.: Princeton University Press, 1949.

Chapin, Stuart, *Cultural Change.* New York: The Century Company, 1928.

Chase Stuart, *The Proper Study of Mankind: An Inquiry into the Science of Human Relations.* New York: Harper & Row, Publishers, 1948, 1956.

————, *Roads to Agreement.* New York: Harper & Row, Publishers, 1951.

Childe, V. Gordon, *Man Makes Himself.* New York: The New American Library, 1951.

————, *Society and Knowledge.* New York: Harper & Row, Publishers, 1956.

Chinoy, Ely, "Social Mobility Trends in the United States," *American Sociological Review,* 20:180–186 (April, 1955).

————, *Society: An Introduction to Sociology.* New York: Random House, 1961.

Clarke, David H., "Social Status and Mental Health of Boys as Related to Their Maturity, Structural Characteristics and Muscular Strength", Unpublished Doctoral Dissertation, University of Oregon, 1960.

Clarke, Harrison and Walter H. Green, "Relationships Between Personal-Social Measures Applied to 10 Year Old Boys," *Research Quarterly,* 34:288–298 (October, 1963).

Clinard, Marshall Brown, *Sociology of Deviant Behavior.* New York: Holt, Rinehart & Winston, Inc., 1963.

Coleman, James S., *The Adolescent Society.* New York: Free Press of Glencoe, Inc., 1961.

Commager, Henry Steele, *Living Ideas in America.* New York: Harper & Row, Publishers, 1951.

Cook, Lloyd Allen, and Elaine F. Cook, *A Sociological Approach to Education* (2nd ed.). New York: McGraw-Hill Book Company, 1950.

Cooley, Charles H., *Human Nature and the Social Order.* New York: Charles Scribner's Sons, 1902.

————, *Social Organization.* New York: Charles Scribner's Sons, 1920.

Coon, Carleton S., *The Story of Man,* rev. ed. New York: Alfred A. Knopf, Inc., 1962.

Coser, Lewis A., and Bernard Rosenberg, *Sociological Theory*. New York: The Macmillan Company, 1964.

———, *The Functions of Social Conflict*. New York: Free Press of Glencoe, Inc., 1956.

Cottrell, Leonard S., "Adjustment of the Individual to His Age and Sex Roles," *American Sociological Review*, 7:617–620 (October, 1942).

Cowell, Charles, "Contributions of Physical Activity to Social Development," *Child Development Abstracts and Bibliography*, 35:190 (October–December), 1961.

Cowell, Charles C., "Validating an Index of Social Adjustment for High School Use," *Research Quarterly*, 29:7–18 (March 1958).

———, Arthur S. Daniels, and Harold E. Kenney, "Purposes in Physical Education as Evaluated by Participants, Physical Education Supervisors, and Educational Administrators," *Research Quarterly*, 22:286–297 (October, 1951).

———, and A. H. Ismail, "Relationships Between Selected Social and Physical Factors," *Research Quarterly*, 33:40–43 (March, 1962).

———, "Validity of a Football Rating Scale and Its Relationship to Social Integration and Academic Ability," *Research Quarterly*, 32:461–467 (December, 1961).

Cozens, Frederick W., and Florence Stumpf, "Implications of Cultural Anthropology for Physical Education," *American Academy of Physical Education, Professional Contributions*, No. 1, 1951.

———, *Sports in American Life*. Chicago: University of Chicago Press, 1953.

Cuber, John Frank, *Sociology, A Synopsis of Principles* (3rd ed.). New York: Appleton-Century-Crofts, 1947, 1955.

———, and William F. Kenkel, *Social Stratification in the United States*. New York: Appleton-Century-Crofts, 1954.

Davis, Kingsley, *Human Society*. New York: The Macmillan Company, 1949.

Davis, Kingsley, and William E. Moore, "Some Principles of Stratification," *American Sociological Review*, 10:242–249 (April, 1945).

DeCharms, Richard, and Prafulachandra N. Dave, "Hope of Success, Fear of Failure, Subjective Probability, and Risk Taking Behavior," *Journal of Personality and Social Psychology*, 1:558–568 (June, 1965).

Denney, Reuel, *The Astonished Muse*. Chicago: University of Chicago Press, 1947.

Dodson, Dan W., "The Integration of Negroes in Baseball," *Journal of Educational Sociology*, 28:73–82 (October, 1954).

Dollard, John, *et al.*, *Frustration and Aggression*. New Haven, Conn. Yale University Press, 1939.

Dubin, Robert, *Human Relations in Administration*. Englewood Cliffs, N.J.: Prentice-Hall, Inc., 1951.

Dulles, Foster Rhea, *America Learns to Play*. New York: Appleton-Century-Crofts, 1940.

Dynes, Russel R., Alfred C. Clarke, and Simon Dinitz, "Levels of Occupational Aspiration: Some Aspects of Family Experience as a Variable," *American Sociological Review*, 21:212–215 (April, 1956).

Eaton, Joseph W., "A Conceptual Theory of Co-operation," *American Journal of Sociology*, 54:126–134 (1948).

Eldridge, Seba, *Fundamentals of Sociology: A Situational Analysis*. New York: Crowell, Collier and Macmillan, Inc., 1950.

Ellis, Robert A., and W. Clayton Lane, "Structural Supports for Upward Mobility," *American Sociological Review*, 28:743–756 (October, 1963).

Farir, Robert E. L., "Development of the Small-Group Research Movement," Chap. 7 in Muzafer Sherif, and M. O. Wilson (eds), *Group Relations at the Crossroads*. New York: Harper & Row, Publishers, 1953.

—— (ed.), *Handbook of Modern Sociology*. Chicago: Rand McNally & Co., 1964.

Faris, Ellsworth, *Discipline without Punishment*. Salt Lake City, Utah: University of Utah Press, 1952.

——, "The Primary Groups: Essence and Accident," *American Journal of Sociology*, 38:41–50 (July, 1932).

Festinger, Leon, Stanley Schacter, and Kurt Back, *Social Pressures in Informal Groups*. New York: Harper & Row, Publishers, 1950.

Firth, Raymond W., *Elements of Social Organization* (3rd ed.). Boston: Beacon Press, 1963.

Freeman, Ellis, *Social Psychology*. New York: Holt, Rinehart & Winston, Inc., 1936.

Freud, Sigmund, *Civilization and Its Discontents*. Translated by Joan Riviere. New York: Ballou, 1930.

Furfey, Paul H., *The Scope and Method of Sociology*. New York: Harper & Row, Publishers, 1953.

Gerth, Hans, and C. Wright Mills, *Character and Social Structure*. New York: Harcourt, Brace & World, Inc., 1953.

Gilfillan, S. C., "Social Implications of Technical Advance," *Current Sociology*, 1:191–207. Paris: UNESCO (1953).

Gillin, John (ed.), *For a Science of Social Man, Convergences in Anthropology, Psychology and Sociology*. New York: The Macmillan Company, 1954.

Gillin, John P., *The Ways of Men*. New York: Appleton-Century-Crofts, 1948.

Ginsberg, Morris, "Social Change," *British Journal of Sociology*, 9:205–229 (September, 1958).

Gittler, Joseph Bertram, *Review of Sociology: Analysis of a Decade*. New York: John Wiley & Sons, Inc., 1957.

Gittler, Joseph P., *Social Dynamics*. New York: McGraw-Hill Book Company, 1952.

Goldschmidt, Walter Rochs, *Man's Way: A Preface to the Understanding of Human Society*. Cleveland, Ohio: World Publishing Company, 1959.

Goldstein, M. J., "The Social Desirability Variable in Attitude Research," *Journal of Social Psychology*, 52:103–108 (August, 1960).

Gordon, Milton M., *Assimilation in American Life*. New York: Oxford University Press, 1964.

Gouldner, Alvin W., *Studies in Leadership*. New York: Harper & Row, Publishers, 1950.

——, and Helen P. Gouldner, *Modern Sociology: Introduction to the Study of Human Interaction*. New York: Harcourt, Brace & World, Inc., 1963.

Graham, Saxon, *American Culture*. New York: Harper & Row, Publishers, 1956.

Green, Arnold W., *Sociology: An Analysis of Life in Modern Society* (2nd ed.). New York: McGraw-Hill Book Company, 1956.

Guetzkow, Harold (ed.), *Groups, Leadership and Men*. Pittsburgh, Penn.: Carnegie Press, 1951.

Guhl, A. M., "The Social Order of Chickens," *Scientific American*, 43–44 (February, 1956).

Gulick, Luther Halsey, *A Philosophy of Play*. New York: Charles Scribner's Sons, 1920.

Gurvitch, Georges, and Wilbert E. Moore, *Twentieth Century Sociology*. New York: Philosophical Library, 1945.

Hallowell, A. Irvin, *Culture and Experience*. Philadelphia: University of Pennsylvania Press, 1955.

———, "Personality Structure and the Evolution of Man," *American Anthropologist*, 52:159–173 (1950).

Handy, Rollo, *Methodology of the Behavioral Sciences*. Springfield, Ill.: Charles C. Thomas, Publisher, 1964.

Harding, D. W., *Social Psychology and Individual Values*. London: Hutchinson and Co., Ltd., 1953.

Hare, A. Paul, Edgar F. Borgotta, and Robert F. Bales, *Small Groups: Studies in Social Interaction*. New York: Alfred A. Knopf, Inc., 1955.

Hart, Hornell, *The Technique of Social Progress*. New York: Holt, Rinehart & Winston, Inc., 1931.

Haskins, Caryl Parker, *Of Societies and Men.* New York: W. W. Norton & Company, Inc., 1951.

Hauser, Richard, and Hephzibah Hauser, *The Fraternal Society*. New York: Random House, 1963.

Havighurst, Robert J., "The Leisure Activities of the Middle-Aged," *The American Journal of Sociology*, 63:152–162 (1957).

———, and Kenneth Feigenbaum. "Leisure and Life-Style," *The American Journal of Sociology*, 64:396–404, January, 1959.

———, and Bernice L. Neugarten, *Society and Education*. Boston: Allyn and Bacon, Inc., 1957.

Hawkes, Glenn R., "A Study of the Personal Values of Elementary School Children," *Educational and Psychological Measurement*, 12:654–663 (Winter, 1952).

———, and John W. Loy, "Toward a Sociology of Sport," *Journal of Health, Physical Education and Recreation*, 36:24–25 (May, 1965).

Hawley, A. H., *Human Ecology: A Theory of Community Structure*. New York: The Ronald Press Company, 1950.

Helanko, R., "Sports and Socialization," *Acta Sociologica*, 2:229–240 (1957).

Herrick, C. Judson, *The Evolution of Human Nature*. Austin: University of Texas Press, 1956.

Herskovits, Melville Jean, *Cultural Anthropology*. New York: Alfred A. Knopf, Inc., 1955.

———, *Man and His Works*. New York: Alfred A. Knopf, Inc., 1948.

Hickman, John A. "Social Class, Attitude Toward Physical Activity, and the Physical Activity of College Students." Unpublished Master's Thesis, University of Wisconsin, 1963.

Hodge, Robert W., Paul M. Siegal, and Peter H. Ross, *Occupational Prestige in the United States*. Chicago: National Opinion Research Center, University of Chicago, 1964, Table I.

Hoebel, Edward Adamson, *Man in the Primitive World: An Introduction to Anthropology*. New York: McGraw-Hill Book Company, 1958.

Homans, George C., "A Conceptual Scheme for the Study of Social Organization," *American Sociological Review*, 12:13–26 (February, 1947).

———, *The Human Group*. New York: Harcourt, Brace & World, Inc., 1950.

———, "Social Behavior as Exchange," *American Journal of Sociology*, 63:597–606 (May, 1958).

———, *Social Behavior in Elementary Forms*. New York: Harcourt, Brace & World, Inc., 1961.

Honigmann, John Joseph, *Understanding Culture*. New York: Harper & Row, Publishers, 1963.

Hood, Albert, "A Study of the Relationship Between Physique and Personality Variables Measured by the MMPI," *Journal of Personality*, 31:97–107 (March (1963).

Horowitz, Irving L., "Consensus, Conflict and Cooperation," *Social Forces*, 41: 177–188 (December, 1962).

Huizinga, Johan, *Homo Ludens: A Study of the Play-Element in Culture*. Boston: Beacon Press, 1950.

Hunter, F., *Community Power Structure*. Chapel Hill: University of North Carolina Press, 1953.

Inkeles, Alex, *What is Sociology*. Englewood Cliffs, N.J.: Prentice-Hall, Inc., 1964.

Ireland, Ralph R., "The Significance of Recreational Maturation in The Education Process: The Six Ages of Play," *Journal of Educational Sociology*, 32:356–360 (March, 1959).

Jaeger, Gertrude, and Philip Selznick, "A Normative Theory of Culture," *American Sociological Review*, 29:653–669 (October, 1964).

Jennings, Helen H., *Leadership and Isolation* (2nd ed.). New York: Longmans, Green & Company, Ltd., 1950.

Johnson, Harry Morton, *Sociology: A Systematic Introduction*. New York: Harcourt, Brace & World, Inc., 1960.

Kahl, Joseph A., *The American Class Structure*. New York: Holt, Rinehart & Winston, Inc., 1956.

Kaplan, Bert, "Personality and Social Structure," Chap. 4 in Joseph B. Gittler, *Review of Sociology*. New York: John Wiley & Sons, Inc., 1957.

Kardiner, Abram, Ralph Linton, *et al.*, *The Psychological Frontiers of Society*. New York: Columbia University Press, 1945.

Kenyon, Gerald S., and John W. Loy, "Toward a Sociology of Sport," *Journal of Health, Physical Education and Recreation*, XXXVI (May 1965), 24–25.

Kenyon, Gerald S., "Sport Sociology: On Becoming a Sub-Discipline," Paper Presented at the American Association for Health, Physical Education and Recreation Convention, March 18, 1966.

Kluckhohn, Clyde, *Culture and Behavior*. New York: Free Press of Glencoe, Inc., 1961.

——, "The Story of Culture" in Coser, Lewis, and Bernard Rosenburg, *Sociological Theory*. New York: The Macmillan Company, 1957.

——, and Henry A. Murray, *Personality in Nature, Society and Culture* (2nd ed.). New York: Alfred A. Knopf, Inc., 1954.

Koenig, Samuel, *Man and Society: The Basic Teachings of Sociology*. New York: Barnes & Noble, Inc., 1957.

Kroeber, A. L., *Anthropology*. New York: Harcourt, Brace & World, Inc., 1948.

——, *Configuration of Cultural Growth*. Berkeley: University of California Press, 1944.

——, *The Nature of Culture*. Chicago: University of Chicago Press, 1952.

——, "The Superorganic," *American Anthropologist* (N.S.), 19:163–213 (April-June, 1917).

Kronenberger, Louis, *Company Manners: A Cultural Inquiry into American Life*. New York: Bobbs-Merrill Company, Inc., 1954.

Landis, Paul Henry, *Introductory Sociology*. New York: The Ronald Press Company, 1958.

LaPiere, Richard T., *A Theory of Social Control*. New York: McGraw-Hill Book Company, 1954.

LaPlace, John P., "Personality and Its Relationship to Success in Professional Baseball," *Research Quarterly*, 25:313–319 (October, 1954).

Lasswell, Thomas E., *Class and Stratum*. Boston: Houghton Mifflin Company, 1965.

Laulicht, Jerome, "Role Conflict," *Social Forces*, 33, No. 3 (March, 1955).

Lee, Joseph, *Play in Education*. New York: National Recreation Association, 1942.

Levy, Marion J., *The Structure of Society*. Princeton, N.J.: Princeton University Press, 1952.

Lewin, Kurt, *Resolving Social Conflicts*. New York: Harper & Row, Publishers, 1948.

Linton, Ralph, *The Study of Man*. New York: Appleton-Century-Crofts, 1936.

———, *The Tree of Culture*. New York: Alfred A. Knopf, Inc., 1955.

Lippitt, R. J. Watson, and B. Westley, *The Dynamics of Planned Change*. New York: Harcourt, Brace & World, Inc., 1958.

Lipset, Seymour M., and Leo Lowenthal (eds), *Culture and Social Character*. New York: Free Press of Glencoe, Inc., 1961.

Loomis, Charles P., *Social Systems: Essays on their Persistence and Change*. Princeton, N.J.: D. Van Nostrand Co., Inc., 1960.

Long, Norton E., "The Local Community as an Ecology of Games," *The American Journal of Sociology*, 64:251–261 (November, 1958).

Lowie, Robert H., *Culture and Ethnology*. New York: R. R. Smith, 1929.

Lowie, Robert, *Social Organizations*. New York: Holt, Rinehart & Winston, Inc., 1948.

Loy, John W., Jr., "Sport and Social Structure," Paper presented at the American Association for Health, Physical Education and Recreation Convention, March 18, 1966.

Lundberg, George Andrew, Clarence C. Schrag, and Otto N. Larsen, *Sociology* (3rd ed.), New York: Harper & Row, Publishers, 1963.

Lynd, R. S., *Middletown*. New York: Harcourt Brace & World, Inc., 1929.

McGraw, L. W., and J. W. Tolbert, "Sociometric Status and Athletic Ability of Junior High School Boys," *Research Quarterly*, 24:72–80 (March, 1953).

McIntosh, P. C., *Sport in Society*. London: C. A. Watts and Company, Ltd., 1963.

MacIver, Robert, *Social Causation*. Boston: Ginn and Company, 1942.

———, *Society: A Textbook of Sociology*. New York: Farrar, Straus & Giroux, Inc., 1937.

Madge, John H., *The Origins of Scientific Sociology*. New York: Free Press of Glencoe, Inc., 1962.

Malinowski, Bronislav, *The Dynamics of Cultural Change*. New Haven: Yale University Press, 1945.

———, *A Scientific Theory of Culture*. Chapel Hill: The University of North Carolina Press, 1944.

Mannheim, Karl, *Freedom, Power and Democratic Planning*. New York: Oxford University Press, Inc., 1950.

March, James G., and Herbert Simon, *Organizations*. New York: John Wiley & Sons, Inc., 1958.

Martindale, Don, *Social Life and Cultural Change*. Princeton, N.J.: D. Van Nostrand Co., Inc., 1962.

Maslow, A. H., *Motivation and Personality*. New York: Harper & Row, Publishers, 1955.

Matthias, Eugene, *The Deeper Meaning of Physical Education.* Translated by Carl L. Schrader. New York: A. S. Barnes and Company, 1929.

May, M. A., and L. U. Doob, *Competition and Cooperation.* New York: Social Science Research Council, 1937, Bulletin 25.

Mead, Eugene, and Fanchon Mead, *Man Among Men.* Englewood Cliffs, N.J.: Prentice-Hall, Inc., 1965.

Mead, Margaret, *Competition and Cooperation among Primitive Peoples.* New York: McGraw-Hill Book Company, 1937.

————, *Male and Female.* New York: William Morrow & Co., Inc., 1949.

Menninger, Karl, *Love Against Hate.* New York: Harcourt, Brace & World, Inc., 1942.

Mercer, Blaine E., *The Study of Society.* New York: Harcourt Brace & World, Inc., 1958.

————, and Edwin R. Carr, *Education and the Social Order.* New York: Holt, Rinehart & Winston, Inc., 1957.

Merrill, Francis Ellsworth, *Society and Culture: An Introduction to Sociology* (3rd ed.). Englewood Cliffs, N.J.: Prentice-Hall, Inc., 1965.

Merton, Robert K., *Social Theory and Social Structure.* New York: Free Press of Glencoe, Inc., 1964.

————, Leonard Broom, and Leonard S. Cottrell, Jr. (eds.), *Sociology Today.* New York: Basic Books, Inc., 1959.

Merz, Charles, *The Great American Bandwagon.* New York: Garden City Publishing Company, Inc., 1928.

Metheny, Eleanor, *Connotations of Movement in Sport and Dance.* Dubuque, Iowa: William C. Brown Company, 1965.

Mills, C. Wright, *The Sociological Imagination.* New York: Oxford University Press, Inc., 1959.

————, *White Collar: The American Middle Class.* New York: Oxford University Press, Inc., 1951.

Miyamoto, S. Frank, and Sanford M. Dornbusch, "A Test of Interactionist Hypothesis of Self Conception," *American Journal of Sociology,* 61:399–403 (March, 1956).

Montague, M. F. Ashley, *On Being Human.* New York: Henry Schuman, 1950.

————, *An Introduction of Physical Anthropology.* New York: Charles C Thomas, 1951.

Moore, Clyde B., and William E. Cole, *Sociology in Educational Practice.* Boston: Houghton Mifflin Company, 1952.

Moore, Omar K., and Alan R. Anderson, "Some Puzzling Aspects of Social Interaction," *The Review of Metaphysics,* 15 (March, 1962).

Moore, Wilbert E., "A Reconsideration of Theories of Social Change," *American Sociological Review,* 25:810–818 (December, 1960).

————, "But Some are More Equal than Others," *American Sociological Review,* 28:13–18 (February, 1963).

————, *Man, Time and Society.* New York: John Wiley & Sons, Inc., 1963.

————, *Social Change.* Englewood Cliffs, N.J.: Prentice-Hall, Inc., 1963.

Mott, Paul E., *The Organization of Society.* Englewood Cliffs, N.J.: Prentice-Hall, Inc., 1965.

Murdock, G., *Outline of Cultural Materials.* New Haven, Conn.: Human Relations Area Files, Inc., 1950.

Myrdal, Gunnar, *An American Dilemma: The Negro Problem and Modern Democracy.* New York: Harper & Row, Publishers, 1944.

Newcomb, Theodore M., "Role Behaviors in the Study of Individual Personality and of Groups," *Journal of Personality* (March, 1950).

———, "Stationary and Changing Societies," *American Journal of Sociology,* 42:16–31 (June, 1936).

Ogburn, William F., "Culture Lag as Theory," *Sociology and Social Research,* 41:167–74 (January-February, 1957).
———, "How Technology Changes Society," *Annals of the American Academy of Political and Social Science,* 249:81–88 (January, 1947).
———, *Social Change.* New York: The Viking Press, Inc., 1950.
———, and Meyer F. Nimkoff, *Sociology* (4th ed.). Boston: Houghton-Mifflin Company, 1964.
Olmstead, Michael S., *The Small Group.* New York: Random House, 1959.

Park, Robert E., and Ernest W. Burgess, *Introduction to the Science of Sociology.* Chicago: University of Chicago Press, 1924.
Parsons, Talcott, "An Analytical Approach to the Theory of Social Stratification," *American Journal of Sociology,* 45:841–62 (May, 1940).
———, *The Social System.* New York: Free Press of Glencoe, Inc., 1951.
Piaget, Jean, *The Moral Judgment of the Child.* Translated by Marjorie Gabain. New York: Harcourt, Brace & World, Inc., 1932.

Quinn, James A., *Human Ecology.* Englewood Cliffs, N.J.: Prentice-Hall, Inc., 1950.

Rarick, L. G., and R. McKee, "A Study of Twenty Third-Grade Children Exhibiting Extreme Levels of Achievement on Tests of Motor Proficiency," *Research Quarterly,* 20:142–152 (May, 1949).
Reaney, M. Jane, "The Correlation Between General Intelligence and Play Ability as Shown in Organized Group Games," *British Journal of Psychology,* 7:226–252 (1914).
Redl, Fritz, "Ten Types of Group Formation," in Coser, Lewis A., and Bernard Rosenberg, *Sociological Theory: A Book of Readings.* New York: The Macmillan Company, 1957.
Riemer, Svend, "Personality," in Roucek, Joseph S. (ed.), *Contemporary Sociology.* New York: Philosophical Library, 1958.
Riesman, David, *Individualism Reconsidered.* New York: Free Press of Glencoe, Inc., 1954.
———, (with Reuel Denney and Nathan Glazer), *The Lonely Crowd.* New Haven: Yale University Press, 1950, 1961.
———, (with Nathan Glazer), *Faces in the Crowd.* New Haven: Yale University Press, 1953.
Roberts, John M., Malcolm J. Arth, and Robert R. Bush, "Games in Culture," *American Anthropologist,* 61:597–605 (August, 1959).
Rose, Arnold Marshall, *Sociology: The Study of Human Relations.* New York: Alfred A. Knopf, Inc., 1956.
Rosen, Bernard, "The Achievement Syndrome: A Psycho-Cultural Dimension of Social Stratification," *American Sociological Review,* 21:202–211 (April, 1956).
———, "Race, Ethnicity, and the Achievement Syndrome," *American Sociological Research,* 24:47–60 (February, 1959).
Rugoff, Natalie, "Local Social Structure and Educational Selection," in A. H. Halsey, *et al.* (eds.), *Education, Economy and Society.* New York: Free Press of Glencoe, Inc., 1951.
Rumney, Jay, and Joseph Maier, *Sociology, The Science of Society.* New York: H. Schuman, 1953.

Sanyal, Batuk Sasadhar, *Culture, An Introduction.* New York: Asia Publishing House, 1962.

Scheinfeld, Amram, *Men and Women.* New York: Harcourt, Brace & World, Inc., 1943.

Sewell, William H., "Social Class and Childhood Personality," *Sociometry,* 24: 340–356 (December, 1961).

Shapiro, Harry L. (ed.), *Man, Culture and Society.* New York: Oxford University Press, Inc., 1956.

Shaw, Marvin, "Some Motivational Factors in Cooperation and Competition," *Journal of Personality,* 26:155–169 (June, 1958).

Sheldon, William, and S. S. Stevens, *The Varieties of Temperament.* New York: Harper & Row, Publishers, 1942.

Sherif, Muzafer, "Subordinate Goals in the Reduction of Intergroup Conflict," *The American Home Journal of Sociology,* 63:349–356 (January, 1948).

———, and Caroline W. Sherif, *Groups in Harmony and Tension.* New York: Harper & Row, Publishers, 1953.

Shubik, Martin, *Game Theory and Related Approaches to Social Behavior.* New York: John Wiley & Sons, Inc., 1964.

Shugart, George, "The Play History: Its Application and Significance," *Journal of Psychiatric Social Work,* 24:204–209 (September, 1955).

Simpson, George, *Man in Society: Studies in Sociology.* New York: Random House, 1954.

Slotkin, J. S., *Social Anthropology.* New York: The Macmillan Company, 1950.

Smelser, N. J., *Theory of Collective Behavior.* New York: Free Press of Glencoe, Inc., 1963.

Sorokin, Pitirim A., *Fads and Foibles in Modern Sociology and Related Sciences:* Chicago: Henry Regnery Co., 1956.

———, *Social Mobility.* New York: Harper & Row Publishers, 1947.

Spengler, Oswald, *The Decline of the West.* New York: Alfred A. Knopf, Inc., 1945.

Start, K. B., "Group Interaction and Examination Results," *Physical Education* (London), 55: No. 166 (November, 1963).

Steiner, Jesse Frederick, *Americans at Play.* New York: McGraw-Hill Book Company, 1933.

Steward, J. H., *Theory of Culture Change.* Urbana: University of Illinois Press, 1955.

Stone, G. P. "Some Meanings of American Sport," Sixteenth Annual Proceedings, CPEA, Columbus, Ohio 6–29 (1957).

Stonequist, E. H., *The Marginal Man.* New York: Charles Scribner's Sons, 1937.

Straus, Murray A., "Deferred Gratification, Social Class and the Achievement Syndrome," *American Sociological Review,* 27:326–335 (June, 1942).

Strauss, Anselm L., *Mirrors and Masks: The Search for Identity.* New York: Free Press of Glencoe, Inc., 1959.

Strunsky, Simeon, *The Living Tradition.* New York: Doubleday and Company, Inc., 1939.

Sugerman, A. Aythur, and Frank Haronian, "Body Type and Sophistication of Body Concept," *Journal of Personality,* 32:380–393 (September, 1964).

Sumner, William Graham, *Folkways.* Boston: Ginn and Company, 1906.

Symonds, Percival M., "Education for the Development of Personality," *Teachers College Record,* 50:163–169 (December, 1948).

Terman, Lewis M., and C. C. Miles, *Sex and Personality: Studies in Masculinity and Femininity.* New York: McGraw-Hill Book Company, 1936.

Thibaut, John W., and Harold H. Kelley, *The Social Psychology of Groups*. New York: John Wiley & Sons, Inc., 1959.

Thrasher, F. M., *The Gang*. Chicago: University of Chicago Press, 1936.

Timasheff, Nicholas S., *Sociological Theory, Its Nature and Growth*. New York: Random House, 1957.

Toynbee, Arnold J., *A Study of History*. Abridgement by D. C. Sommervell. New York: Oxford University Press, Inc., 1946.

Trapp, William G., "A Study of Social Integration in a College Football Squad," *56th Annual Proceedings*. Washington D.C.: College Physical Education Association, 1953.

Tumn, Melvin M., "Some Principles of Stratification: A Critical Analysis," *American Sociological Review*, 18:387–394 (August, 1953).

Tunnis, John, *Sports, Heroics and Hysterics*. New York: The John Day Company, Inc., 1928.

Tyler, E. B., *Primitive Culture* (7th ed.). New York: Brentano's, Inc., 1924.

Valentine, Alan, *The Age of Conformity*. Chicago: Henry Regnery Co., 1954.

Vander Zanden, James W., *Sociology: A Systematic Approach*. New York: The Ronald Press Company, 1965.

Van Waters, Miriam, *Youth in Conflict*. New York: Republic Publishing Company, 1925.

Veblen, Thorstein, *The Theory of the Leisure Class*. New York: Huebsch, 1919.

Walsh, Eleanor A., "The Relationship Between Motor Proficiency and Social Status of Elementary School Girls." Unpublished Master's Thesis, University of Wisconsin, 1955.

Warner, W. Lloyd, *American Life: Dream and Reality*. Chicago: University of Chicago Press, 1953.

———, and Paul S. Lunt, *The Status System of a Modern Community*. New Haven: Yale University Press, 1942.

———, Marchia Meeker, and Kenneth Ells, *Social Class in America*. Chicago: Science Research Associates, 1949.

Wecter, Dixon, *The Hero in America*. New York: Charles Scribner's Sons, 1941.

Weinberg, Meyer, and Oscar E. Shabat, *Society and Man*. Englewood Cliffs, N.J.: Prentice-Hall, Inc., 1965.

Weinberg, S. K., and H. Arond, "The Occupational Culture of the Boxer," The *American Journal of Sociology*, 57:460–469 (March, 1952).

Whetten, Nathan L., and Arnold W. Green, "Field Research and the Concept of Assimilation," *Rural Sociology*, 7:252–260 (1942).

White, Cyril M., "Toward a Sociology of Physical Education and Sport: Some Theoretical Considerations," Paper presented at the American Association for Health, Physical Education and Recreation Convention, March 18, 1966.

White, Leslie A., "Culturological vs. Psychological Interpretations of Human Behavior," *American Sociological Review*, 12:686–696 (December, 1947).

———, *The Evolution of Culture*. New York: McGraw-Hill Book Company, 1959.

———, *The Science of Culture*. New York: Farrar, Straus & Giroux, Inc., 1949.

Whyte, William F., *Street Corner Society*. Chicago: University of Chicago Press, 1955.

Wilensky, Harold L., and Hugh Edwards, "The Skidder: Ideological Adjustments of Downward Mobile Workers," *American Sociological Review*, 24:215–231 (April, 1959).

Williams, Robin M., *American Society* (rev. ed.). New York: Alfred A. Knopf, Inc., 1960.

————, *The Reduction of Intergroup Tensions.* New York: Social Science Research Council, 1947.

Wolff, Kurt H. (ed.), *The Sociology of George Simmel.* New York: Free Press of Glencoe, Inc., 1950.

Wood, Mary Margaret, *Path of Loneliness.* New York: Columbia University Press, 1953.

Worrell, Leonard, "The Preference for Conflict: Some Paradoxical Reinforcement Effects," *Journal of Personality,* 32:32–44 (March, 1964).

Young, Kimball, and Raymond W. Mack, *Sociology and Social Life.* New York: American Book Company, 1965.

Yukie, E. C., "Group Movement in a Physical Education Class," *Research Quarterly,* 26:222–233 (May, 1955).

Znaniecki, Florian, *Social Actions.* New York: Holt, Rinehart & Winston, Inc., 1936.

Index